To: T

With my compliments,

Terry

Dec. 14, 1992

New York

THROUGH MY EYES

THROUGH MY EYES

Wall Street, Washington, D.C., and Japan's Diet

Yoshio Terasawa

The Japan Times

First edition, December 1992

Cover design by Kumiko Hamilton
Editorial supervision and book design by Stephen Comee

For information, write: The Japan Times, Ltd.,
4-5-4 Shibaura, Minato-ku, Tokyo 108, Japan.

ISBN 4-7890-0666-2

Published in Japan by the Japan Times, Ltd

PRINTED IN JAPAN

Contents

Part One: Encountering America

Preface

This book was published to serve the cause of international friendship. In these times of ever-mounting global friction, I am convinced that we must confront a growing need for global understanding among our earth's peoples. In the hope that my experiences may contribute something to international understanding, I present this book as my gift to you.

As the appropriately vague title suggests, this book is about everything and, some might say, nothing in particular. *Through My Eyes* is a collection of assorted short articles I have written over the years for Japanese newspaper and magazine audiences. The topics range from my childhood memories of postwar Japan to my impressions of power on Wall Street and parties on Capitol Hill, and cover just about everything else in between. My purpose in making these writings available in English is to show the people of the world what it is like to work in a foreign land, and to make friends with people from all over the world. I want to share with them my view of America from the interesting positions I have held—from my dormitory at Wharton, to my desk at Nomura Securities on Wall Street, to my office at the World Bank's Multilateral Investment Guarantee Agency (MIGA) in Washington, and finally to my senatorial post in Japanese government. This is a book about my work and travels, but much more than that, it is a book about what my work and travels have come to mean to me in terms of human relationships.

I have lived for more than twenty years in the United States, but my love affair with America had very humble beginnings.

Fresh out of Waseda University, I discovered that even a person with my grades could gain acceptance to the prestigious Nomura Securities with a bit of résumé-padding. My "fluent English skills" got me the job, but I didn't expect to be sent to America so soon! Part One of this book describes the joys and trials of "Encountering America."

Shortly after my acceptance into Nomura, I received a Fulbright scholarship and began my life in America at the Graduate Division of the University of Pennsylvania's Wharton School. My experiences there make up the bulk of Chapter 1. I was lucky to meet good people and made many good friends during that time.

Chapter 2 continues the saga of my encounter with the U.S. by describing what happened to me over the next several years. When my studies at Wharton were finished, I was transferred to Nomura's New York branch and became a stockbroker on Wall Street. My work there put me in close contact with American ways of doing business, and also gave me a clearer view of my own country and its policies. Eventually, I became a member of the New York Stock Exchange—where my registration number was 1620, the year the *Mayflower* reached America—certainly, I believed, an auspicious number for the first Japanese pilgrim on the U.S. stock-market scene.

But not all my memories of New York are business-related, as Chapter 3 shows. I also interacted with a number of people far too numerous to have included in this book. Many not found in these pages were very close to me, and many of them are no longer of this world. But the ones found here all taught me something of what it is to be a friend, of what it means to be human—something that none of us should ever forget.

Part Two describes "Life in Washington," and is a diary of my stay in the U.S. Many of the episodes are stories involving personal friends. That is not to say that my work at MIGA did not teach me new lessons about Japanese-American styles of business; rather, this selection demonstrates how personal a place

Washington can be if you let yourself enjoy the city and its people.

Chapter 6 is a collection on my thoughts about the future, and Chapter 7 introduces thoughts gleaned during my travels to other lands. The more I travel abroad, and the more I carry on intimate business with economic powerhouses around the world, the more I see that it is not so much a matter of them vs. us but a question of mutual acceptance. It is people, not political machines, that make the world go round.

Part Three conveys "Life in Japan," both before and after I had returned to Japan for good. Chapter 8 discusses some of the adjustments I had to make to "fit back in," and Chapter 9 is something that was added just as this book was in preparation—it is a diary of my whirlwind decision to run and the resulting campaign leading to my election to the Upper House of Japan's National Diet.

I should warn you in advance that I am fond of writing from the hip. My Japanese readers find this characteristic endearing, and so I hope you will too. You may occasionally feel as if I am repeating myself from one section to the next. I assure you that this is not due (entirely) to senility, but rather to the nature of writing magazine columns. Bear with me; I am certain, or at the very least hopeful, that my words will stimulate and provoke. And if this book helps even one person to gain better insight into international relations or to understand that we all share a common humanity that we must preserve at any cost, then my efforts will have been well worthwhile. . .

I would like to take this opportunity to thank all of the people who were so instrumental in bringing about the publication of this book. First of all, I would like to thank Mr. Toshiaki Ogasawara, long-time friend and Chairman of the Japan Times, who kindly advised me to publish this book. There are far too many others to name individually—but they know who they are, and I thank them sincerely. Special thanks are due to two women without whose assistance this book would never have seen the light of day, Ms. Fujiko Hara and Ms. Yoshiko Nagano, as well as to my two excellent editors, two of my wonderful former secretaries, Ms. Dian Simpson and Ms. Celia Koenig, and Mr. Stephen Comee, an expatriate American working in Japan as both an editor/designer and business consultant. Thanks are also due to Mr. Masayuki Ishida of the Japan Times publications department and to Mr. Brandon Lucas, a young American secretary to Congressman Koki Kobayashi, for their unstinting help and assistance.

November 1992
Tokyo

Part One

Encountering America

1

School Days

Why Did I Think of Studying Abroad?

In 1954, upon graduation from Waseda University, I joined Nomura Securities. By chance, I was assigned to the foreign division. Well, almost by chance, because I did have the chutzpah to write on my resume that English was my strongest school subject, and that I could even act as an interpreter. It was a slight exaggeration that I had to use in order to get a job at Nomura Securities, which would have been unattainable for someone like myself who had no personal connections or other advantages. The Korean War had ended in 1953, followed by the "Stalin Market Crash," and I graduated the very next year. It was a hard time for students of my generation who had to begin looking for jobs in September of 1953.

"You say here that you are proficient in spoken English, and can act as an interpreter, too. Is that true? If you were at the counter and an American client came in, would you be able to do business right away?" a Nomura executive asked me. "No, I wouldn't," I replied. "I know English, but right now I don't know the terminology of the securities market. But after I have mastered those terms, maybe in about six months, I will be ready to do business in English."

For all I know, Nomura might have been aware of my lack of competence. They may have hired me because of my nerves of steel! I found my first days in Nomura quite enjoyable.

For the application form that foreign investors had to submit before purchasing Japanese stocks, I inserted three sheets of carbon paper sandwiched among the pages and wrote with a hard-tipped ball-point pen so that the lowermost copy would be clear. In 1952, the Law Concerning Foreign Investment was established, allowing non-residents to buy Japanese stocks for the first time. But even after the enactment of the new law, an application had to be submitted in advance to obtain a remittance guarantee. My first job was to fill out the application forms, and take them to the Bank of Japan by 3 PM to get approval.

When I filled out the forms, the young woman who sat next to me would lean closer in order to help me with this office work, which was entirely new to me. I could feel her warm breath, and my heart beat as if it would explode at any time, but of course she didn't know that. I was lousy at clerical jobs, to start with. How could I write neat application forms in such an atmosphere? Such scenes have now become sweet old memories.

To say that I lost myself in liquor and became a slave to gambling would be an exaggeration, but for a while I did lead a rather wild life. The time came, though, when I told myself, "I cannot go on like this." One day, Mr. Egashira, one of my colleagues, came back from Princeton University. I still remember how his eyes shone with pity when he looked at me. As Mr. Egashira later told me, "At that time, I thought it was the only way to save you. Somebody had to give you a clearer purpose in life. I thought studying abroad would be the best means." Mr. Egashira was extremely helpful. He helped me with all the application procedures for a Fulbright scholarship, and that was how I ended up in Seattle.

Joining Nomura Securities

As I mentioned earlier, I joined Nomura Securities in April 1954, immediately after graduating from Waseda University. On April

1, my first day at the company, I noticed a tall, slim man by the window, reading a book in English. This fair-skinned, handsome man stood rather aloof from the rest of the crowd. He had an academic air about him, sort of like a college professor. I approached him cautiously. He introduced himself as Keisuke Egashira, a graduate of Keio University's Department of Economics. He said, "I came here at the suggestion of my professor at Keio, and will be with you for only two months, since I'm going to Princeton University in June on a Fulbright scholarship." His remarks truly impressed me. At that time, it was a very big deal to study in the United States.

So began my encounter with Keisuke Egashira, who has greatly influenced my life. We were both assigned to the Foreign Division, and we later worked together in the International Division. (Egashira later assumed the post of Managing Director of Nomura Securities, London. He is currently President of J. Osawa & Co., Ltd.)

A Big Slump

"I'm back, Mom!"

"I'm glad you're safely home, Yoshio."

"Yeah, it feels so good to be back. Japan is the best."

I had returned to my old home town of Sano. My mother was there, too.

"I like Japan best," I said, caressing the familiar surface of the tatami mat.

A commotion of people moving . . . what was going on? I awoke, stunned, and remembered where I was. I had dozed off and dreamed about going back to Sano and meeting my mother. Class had just finished. The students around me were putting their notebooks and pencils into their bags.

There, I had done it again! I was determined to be attentive that day, sat in the front row, and tried to listen carefully to the professor's lecture. This is too much! I was again overwhelmed by a feeling of defeat and inferiority. I trudged wearily out of the classroom and sat absentmindedly on a bench.

A squirrel ran up near my feet, and looked up.

I had not been able to sleep well lately, so I often dozed off during class. I could not understand English. Even when I did understand the language, the content was difficult. And it was no fun. Moreover, I did not feel motivated. "What will become of me if I go on like this?" I wondered. I had heard about a student from Japan who suffered a nervous breakdown and was sent back home. Whenever I dozed off in class, I dreamed about my mother and tatami mats.

I remembered a haiku by Kobayashi Issa:

Wareto kite asobeya oyano nai suzume
(Come and play with me, orphan sparrow.)

Somehow the squirrel resembled the sparrow in the poem. Maybe it was the squirrel who was trying to comfort the pitifully depressed student from the Orient.

I started to plod back to the dorm. I stood in front of the milk vending machine, and put a quarter in it. A one-quart carton of milk come down with a thud. People of today might find this hard to understand, but milk was something extremely special to a Japanese of those days, both in terms of quality and quantity. I took the milk back to my room. Winter in Philadelphia was very chilly.

Roasted Rice-balls

What in the world had caused my helpless slump? Was it a

reaction against the sudden change from my easy and care-free life in Japan? Had that made me hate everything in the U.S.? Was I missing too much the girl friend I had left in Japan? I don't know. Anyhow, I felt homesick every day. I wanted to go back to Japan.

It started in my sleep. It was still 11 PM. Another repetition of the vicious cycle . . . But I felt rather hungry. "Why don't I make myself a nice, roasted rice-ball?"

I lived about a thirty-minute walk from the University of Pennsylvania. I had rented the attic room on the third floor of Rev. and Mrs. Jacobses' home. The room had a small sink and a cooking stove in the corner. When I had those sudden cravings for Japanese food, I would try my hand at cooking, which resulted in disaster every time. "How could I possibly succeed in making a properly roasted rice-ball?" I would stare at the shapeless chunk of rice that was the result of my futile effort, and which didn't even look like a rice-ball, and tears came to my eyes despite myself. By then, it was nearly three in the morning. I had a class starting at nine that morning. I knew I would not be able to get any sleep if I went back to bed.

A Shrine for Japanese Students

There is a building in Philadelphia that was named the "Philadelphia Shrine" by the Japanese students of those days. Owned by Mr. and Mrs. Inoue, three out of four floors were rented to students only. Mr. Inoue was a second-generation Japanese-American from California, who had moved from the West Coast to this eastern city. As he was at least in his mid-fifties when I met him, he must have been born in the late 1800s.

I stayed there my first night in Philadelphia. In those days, almost every student from Japan did. We called the Inoue house the Philadelphia Shrine, in the sense that all Japanese students who were visiting Philadelphia or were there to go to school had to go there at least once.

I don't remember very well what Mr. Inoue looked like, but I have a very clear memory of what kind of person Mrs. Inoue was. She was a small woman with refined features, but I remember her most of all for her resolute attitude. She offered me a warm welcome in spite of the fact that I had just walked in without calling in advance. I was shown to a small room in the attic, where Mrs. Inoue changed the sheets on a shabby bed like the kind you find in hospitals.

I only stayed there overnight, and another Japanese student, Mr. Harada from the Ministry of Agriculture, moved in after me. When I grew lonesome living in Rev. Jacobs' attic, I often visited the "Shrine."

Rev. and Mrs. Jacobs were kind, openhearted people. Mrs. Jacobs was a tall, solid-looking, ruddy-cheeked woman who appeared to be of German descent. She told me I should put my trash in a hard, big, brown bag, twist the top and tie it with a piece of string, and put it in the can in front of the house, making sure the large lid was closed.

On my way from downtown Tokyo to Haneda Airport, as I passed Kamata, I could see black wooden garbage-boxes on the streets, lids half open, showing the remains of red watermelons with flies swarming on them. Such sights were common in Japan in those days, so I was quite impressed by the way Americans disposed of the garbage.

On Sunday morning at 6:30 I was woken up by a voice from downstairs calling "Terry! Terry! Wake up!" It was Rev. Jacobs calling me so he could take me to Sunday school at the church. I remember nothing about the Bible, not even the crucial subject-matter, but I can still smell the aroma of the coffee that helped wipe the sleep out of my eyes, and I can almost taste the mild sweetness of the donuts.

After breakfast, he always took me to the church and made me act as an "usher." At the end of the prayer, I handed a basket to the first person in the first row. That person would take a crumpled dollar-bill out of his pocket and put it in the basket, then hand it to the person sitting next to him. This was repeated for each row. Being a materialist who has never believed in any god, I cannot suppress a bitter smile whenever I think back to what I used to do then.

One day, Rev. Jacobs said, "Terry, there's going to be a seminar at Pennsylvania Women's College from the end of this year to the beginning of next year. Why don't you come with me?"

The topic of the seminar was "The Chosen People." There are many different religious groups in the U.S.: Protestants, Catholics, Jews, etc., and each group has the notion that they are God's "Chosen People." So college students representing the different religions from all over the nation were going to gather and hold a thorough debate on the matter.

The day of the seminar, Rev. Jacobs, Nancy and I were driving on the Pennsylvania turnpike from Philadelphia to Pittsburgh at a high speed of 80 mph. Nancy, a petite blonde with a small face and beautiful, round teeth, was a freshman at the Drexel Institute of Technology (which is right next to the University of Pennsylvania).

I had been feeling rather excited from the moment we left Philadelphia that day. I was going to debate as a "Buddhist student," and Nancy as a devout Catholic.

In about five hours, we arrived at Pittsburgh. As I entered the bedroom I was given, I found a stuffed bear sitting on the neatly covered bed. Since it was a women's college, the occupant of this room was of course a young girl. I felt just a little bit awkward about using a girl's bed in her absence, but I lay down on it because I was exhausted.

The discussions in the classroom turned out to be quite serious. With my limited knowledge of English, I could understand only about 30 percent of what was being said. But, being there as a representative of the Buddhist religion, I had to give a speech when it was my turn. "What on earth am I supposed to say?" was my only thought as I waited.

I finally decided to say something like: "The teachings of Buddhism can be summed up in the notion that the world we live in is evanescent, and it is essentially 'nothing.' Therefore, unlike the various Christian denominations, I do not think Buddhists have any notion of being 'God's chosen people.' "

Moving into the Dormitory

After giving it a lot of thought, I decided to move into the dormitory and live with American students. My roommates were Tom and George. Tom had graduated from Notre Dame, George from Princeton, and both were graduate students at the law school.

Yotaro Kobayashi and Osamu Toba were in the same dorm, though our rooms were different. Today, Mr. Kobayashi is Chairman of Fuji-Xerox, and Mr. Toba, President of Morgan Guaranty Trust. These two gentlemen shared the following three characteristics: they were handsome, good at tennis, and good students.

Wharton School had a nasty tradition. After the final examinations of each term, the names of the students were posted on the bulletin board in the hall, in order of the results on the exams. Both Mr. Kobayashi and Mr. Toba's names used to appear in the first, second, or third place from the top; always within the top five. As for me, I got either the booby prize or the booby-maker's prize. I resented this cruel practice. Though my academic performance did improve after moving to the dormitory, I still found it very difficult to keep up.

Thanksgiving

"Autograph, please!"

The moment I stepped into the drugstore, I was surrounded by five or six children. Each of them held out a small note-pad.

"His hair is black, but his eyes are brownish," said a girl about ten years old, talking like a grown-up.

I was visiting a small town called Pottsville in northern Pennsylvania. The local Rotary Club had invited around fifty foreign students for Thanksgiving, via an introduction from a couple of universities in Philadelphia. I participated in the activity as a representative of the Japanese students.

Pottsville is a coal-mining town. Unlike in Japan, where vertical shafts are used for excavating, coal is mined here by strip-mining, which means that the mountain surface is cut. The area is considered a remote corner of the country. The children had gathered to have a look at the dark-eyed Japanese, a rare species around there. I was probably in the same position as the blue-eyed, red-haired "barbarians" from Europe who were stared at with curiosity in old Japan in the sixteenth and seventeenth centuries. It was a funny feeling.

In Pottsville, each of us stayed with a local family for one week. I stayed with Michael, a truck driver. The trucks were much larger than the ones I used to see in Japan. Michael was also a big man, nearly two meters tall. His arms were as big as my legs. One has to be strong to steer those trucks!

Thanksgiving in America resembles the Japanese New Year. Family members gather together from all over the country for the occasion. Christmas is not necessarily like that. In fact, Christmas was celebrated only by Christians, while the people of other religions are totally indifferent to it—except as a time for getting gifts! American New Year's is practically non-existent. Only New Year's Day is a holiday, observed by schools and businesses.

The highlight of Thanksgiving is the turkey. The inside of the turkey is stuffed, and each family has its own special recipe for the "stuffing," just as in Japan the New Year *ozoni* (soup with boiled rice cakes and vegetables) differs from home to home.

Singing "Sanosa"

My life as a student in Philadelphia was a disaster academically speaking, but I did have some interesting experiences. There were various gatherings of groups with such names as the Oaks Club, the Womens' Club, etc. Most were charity organizations whose members were women. After finishing their most important job of raising children, many American women around the age of fifty start to participate in social activities. I was often invited to speak at such clubs.

In the meetings, I used to talk about religion in Japan and about the fact that religion has lost its power in Japan. For instance, if someone passes away, we go to a Buddhist temple. When someone gets married, we go to the Shinto shrine. We have both a family Buddhist altar and a Shinto shrine in our homes. The audience would stare at me in disbelief when I said those things. Just like our reaction to the customs of the American Indians, their impression of Japan seemed to be that it is a "strange" country rather than an "exotic" place.

I usually ended my speech by singing a song called "Sanosa." I wonder how I ever managed to sing in public without feeling any hesitation or embarassment.

2

Wall Street Memories

Joining Nomura Securities

At the urging of Egashira, I had taken the examination for the Fulbright Scholarship. To my surprise, I passed, an incident which for better or worse greatly changed the course of my life.

On August 30, 1956, I climbed on board the *Hikawa-maru,* a Nippon Yusen ship bound for the U.S. I will never forget that day. Fourteen days later, I disembarked in Seattle. By the time I reached Philadelphia, it was September 15, 1956.

I studied at the Wharton School of Business at the University of Pennsylvania until June 30, 1957. After graduation, I was posted to the New York branch through the considerate arrangement of Shoshi Kawashima, Manager of the International Division (later Chairman of Kokusai Securities Co., Ltd.). He thought I should immediately get some on-the-job experience on Wall Street, so I moved from Philadelphia to New York.

Nomura Securities first set up a business office in New York back in 1927. This was only a year after the Securities Division of Nomura Bank (currently Daiwa Bank) became independent and Nomura Securities had been established. That shows how eager the company was to start overseas operations. After World War II, Nomura Securities reopened a New York office in March 1953, ahead of its rivals, and upgraded its business office to branch status soon after that.

When I joined the branch, the offices were located at 61 Broadway and had only three employees: Tadashi Ishida, the branch manager (who succeeded Kawashima), Eiichi Kuwayama, a Japanese-American, and Yoshiko Minejima, the secretary. Eiichi Kuwayama had been born and raised in New York, and had graduated from Princeton University and Harvard Business School. He had worked as an interpreter for Minoru Segawa (Managing Director at the time) during Segawa's visit to the U.S. in 1951. That was the start of his career with Nomura Securites. Kuwayama came to Japan and stayed with the Segawa family while studying finance. He later served as the New York branch manager after Ishida (1957–66).

When I joined the New York branch, I did all the odd jobs. At that time, we had no telex machine, so I would type up an order on a telegram sheet, for example, "Buy Yawata, 5000" and take it to a telegraph office. The next day, a messenger would bring back the answer, "Bought Yawata, 5000, 80 yen." Our correspondence with Japan was mainly by mail. We rarely made overseas calls because they were too expensive, and it took half a day for a call to get through to Japan.

For employees posted abroad, I think the invention of the telex machine marked the beginning of the end of their peaceful lives. I would go to the office at nine in the morning to find a telex waiting for me, ordering me to meet Mr. So-and-so or to conduct research on such-and-such a topic. And because of the time difference, I invariably would have to get things done and telexed back on the same day. The good old days were over.

Our initial task at that time was to sell Japanese stocks. We did advertise, but we could afford only a small space in the *New York Times* because of our limited budget. As an eye catcher, we put the word *kabu* (meaning stock in Japanese) in Chinese characters on top, and below that, "Stock, Please Call Nomura Securities" in English. Actually, however, it was not that effective. Japanese stocks just did not sell.

Our other task was to handle dollar-denominated bonds issued in Japan before World War II. Before the war, the City of

Tokyo, Tokyo Dento, and other entities issued government-guaranteed dollar bonds. During the war, the government converted the dollar bonds owned by Japanese investors into yen bonds. But the bonds owned by Americans and Japanese residents in New York were still in dollar denominations even after the war. The Japanese government was in no shape to repay the bonds immediately after the war, so it extended the terms of repayment by ten years. As a means of compensation, the government issued coupons for the ten years' interest. The bonds and interest coupons were being actively traded for the semi-annual interest payments and the discounted price made them quite attractive.

The big three Japanese companies in New York in those days were the Bank of Tokyo (which took over Yokohama Shokin Bank), Mitsui & Co., and Nippon Yusen. Only a handful of Japanese banks had branches in New York: if I remember correctly, just the Bank of Tokyo, and Mitsubishi, Mitsui, and Sumitomo banks.

Nomura Securities International, Inc., now has 670 employees. Sixty-eight employees are from Japan, and the rest are American nationals. It makes me realize how much things have changed over the years. Back in the pioneer days, we used to cut out any newspaper articles we saw on Japan. When you found one, other workers in the office would gather around to read it. Nowadays, there are almost daily articles on Japan, either favorable or unfavorable, in the *New York Times* or the *Wall Street Journal.* When you see a capital "J," you can almost bet the article is about Japan.

Specialists

I visited John Phelan, Chairman of the Board of Directors of the New York Stock Exchange. John is fifty-six, just like myself. His father was a stock specialist as well. The NYSE has many entrances, among which the one on 11 Wall Street is the side door, so to speak. The front door address is actually 20 Broad Street.

Today there are 1,500 stocks listed on the New York exchange. For each stock there is a 'specialist' who handles that particular stock exclusively. There are around four-hundred specialists, each of whom handles four or five stocks. When a member dealer wants to buy an IBM stock, for instance, he goes to the specialist who is in charge of IBM.

Specialists serve two purposes: The first is to match the buy and sell orders of the members. The second is to buy when there are only sells and no buys, and therefore no price, and to sell when there are no sells to match the buys.

To be a specialist one must be somewhat perverse, since the job entails selling when everyone else is buying, and buying when everyone is selling. On the other hand, specialists tend to be wealthy.

The Tokyo Stock Exchange also has an old saying that goes: "On a mountain of flowers, there are back roads behind the roads." Both in the West and in the East, it seems that a somewhat perverse type of investment technique might brings better results.

The offices of Morgan Guaranty are located at the corner of Wall Street and Broad Street. This the headquarters of the famous Morgan financial group. The entrance is at the top of a flight of about ten stone steps from ground level. Once inside the building, you can see an incredibly large chandelier hanging from the ceiling.

Back in 1920, a bomb planted in the building by an anarchist claimed the lives of thirty-three people and wounded four hundred. To this day, the scars of that incident are preserved in the building's walls.

The chairman of this bank is Dennis Weatherstone, an authority on world currencies. Whenever monetary policy authorities in Washington are at their wits' end, they turn to Dennis Weatherstone for advice.

He fits none of the following 'requirements for the chairman' of a large banking institution: being a WASP (white, Anglo-Saxon, Protestant—the minimum requirement for becoming a member of the elite in American financial circles); having a strong, imposing physique; and being a graduate of one of the prestigious Ivy League universities such as Harvard or Princeton.

Instead, he possesses qualities that seem more important than all of the above, especially, a charismatic and attractive personality and knowledge and expertise in his particular field that no one can match. I like him very much and greatly respect him. Three or four pictures of his family decorate his office—not elaborate portraits taken in a photo studio, but very casual snapshots.

The 'President's Office'

Whenever we have a visitor at a company in Japan, it is customary to show him to a separate reception room. In America, the guest is ushered into the president's or the chairman's own office, if that is who they are visiting.

The executive's office is not only decked out with family photos, but filled with all kinds of memorabilia such as hand-carved, native dolls obtained in Africa, a dancer's costume from Indonesia, or porcelain dolls from Hakata, Japan. All this gives you the impression of being in the warmth of his own living room. It is 'his room' rather than 'the president's office.'

In Japan, the Prime Minister's office is the workplace for all prime ministers, whoever they might be. So whether the prime minister is Mr. Tanaka or Mr. Nakasone, the individual is not taken into consideration. It is an office to be used by the whoever happens to have the title of prime minister.

Just as the standard inaugural speech of a new corporate president in Japan starts with the words, "Following the route set by my predecessor, . . ." so the president's office is seldom altered to fit the new occupant's taste.

The U.S. presidential elections are held on the second Tuesday of November every four years. Every new president who occupiesthe White House beginning the following January will probably hammer out a political scheme which departs from his predecessor's line as much as possible. And the new First Lady will tear off the wall-paper of the White House walls and replace it with something new.

Them and Us: How We Differ

Whenever a Japanese visitor to my company leaves, I see him to the elevator. When he is inside the elevator, I say *"Arigato gozaimashita"* (Thank you very much) and make a polite bow. Usually, the elevator is full of other passengers, all American. The door, rather than closing promptly, takes ages to shut. All this time, I keep my head bowed. I wonder if the Americans think I'm crazy, but, on second thought, I tell myself that this is a good old Japanese custom, so I shouldn't worry.

A limousine stops in front of a Japanese restaurant in Manhattan, and group of four or five Japanese who have just come out of the restaurant get in. Another group of three or four, standing on the street outside the car, bow and see the men in the car off. One Japanese in the car promptly rolls down the window and sticks out his head and nods. Another Japanese in the car gestures to the chauffeur, an American, urging him to start the car. The chauffeur, however, seems to think that he should wait as long as the passenger is speaking through the open window. Before long, the cars behind get impatient and start honking their horns, as the street is already getting congested.

A long time ago, I attended a party held at the Waldorf Astoria in honor of a former Japanese bureaucrat who had become president of a large company. Waiting in line, I saw the new president standing in the receiving line bowing. His bows seemed awkward. It was somewhat funny but understandable, as I assumed that the man, having been a bureaucrat for a long time, must have been used to receiving bows from others but not bowing himself. When my turn came, I bowed in front of him, and he lowered his head at exactly the same moment so that we literally had a "head-on" collision. It rather hurt. I felt sorry for him; it must have hurt him, too, since I am a hard-headed person.

Handshaking is to Americans what bowing is to the Japanese. Generally speaking, Americans have large hands, so shaking hands with them sometimes hurts. It must be even more uncomfortable for Japanese women, who have even smaller hands. I heard that Miss Kaoru Kanetaka, whose profession takes her around the world continuously, greets others by clasping their hands as if in a Buddhist monk's prayer, because she finds the Japanese-style of bowing somewhat awkward, but thinks shaking hands is too un-Japanese. I think she has a point.

Traditional Japanese manners and customs are considered "ritualistic" by Americans, who either think they are troublesome, or imitate them for fun. Americans who are undergoing training in *judo* or *kendo* faithfully follow the command "*Rei!* (Bow!)" and they practice hard. In this case, the "ritual" is part of the rhythm required in the training. Tea ceremony and flower arrangement are also made up of a continuous chain of ritualistic acts.

Government Officials vs. Private Citizens

In New York's East River, which is quite a large river, there is an island called Roosevelt Island. It is a residential area, filled with large apartment buildings similar to Japan's housing corporation complexes. About seven or eight years ago, the leader of that community received a letter from the Ministry of Education of Japan, which said: "We would like to introduce the average American's lifestyle to the Japanese public. A few weeks from now, we plan to send a TV production crew and would appreciate your cooperation."

The Japanese TV crew arrived, along with cameras and other equipment. The local people were rather friendly to the Japanese crew and tried to offer whatever assistance they could.

But they were startled to read the weird scenario passed out to them. "The head of the house works at a securities company on Wall Street. The distance between Wall Street and Roosevelt Island is only about six kilometers. At lunch time, the husband comes home. Having replenished his energy by enjoying a home-made meal carefully prepared by his wife, the husband goes back to work."

Roosevelt Island's community leader took the time to explain, very slowly, to the Japanese director, who was not very good at English, the following: "I know it is about six kilometers to Wall Street as the crow flies. But to get there from here, you have to do the following: You first take a bus and a cable tram to go to Manhattan; that takes about fifteen minutes; then you change to the subway to get to Wall Street, which takes thirty minutes. Of course, you have to add to this the walking and waiting time. So, it adds up to almost one hour door-to-door. You can't afford to go home for lunch since it takes two hours for the round trip. Even if someone did go home for lunch, it would be a very simple meal, with each member of the family separately fixing a peanut-butter sandwich for himself, for example. There would be no time for the wife to 'prepare a home-made meal.' "

He explained this repeatedly, but the director would not agree to any changes. The representatives of the community gathered and discussed the matter. The majority felt that since U.S.-Japan relations were already strained to begin with, it wasn't wise to risk an unfavorable impression by refusing to cooperate point-blank. The community who were chosen to be filmed ended up polishing the silverware usually reserved for Thanksgiving or Christmas, changing the dining-room curtains, and being forced into all kinds of extra work.

When the filming was over, the Japanese left the island. But the community leader, who needed to release his frustration in some way, recounted the whole event for the local community paper. "I am not complaining about having to go to the extra trouble of polishing the silverware and redecorating the house, but Americans just don't live life as depicted in the scenario prepared by the Japanese. If the Japanese government has enough money to send a TV production crew to our country, I wish they would film the reality of our everyday life."

Unbelievable as this may sound, it is a true story. I have no idea where that video film is being used.

Insufficient PR on the Part of Japan

America is an interesting place. People hate "government organizations" and are relatively unimpressed by "national" institutions. Totally opposite from Japan, even at the college level, private universities seem to be making their presence felt more than the state universities. National research institutions do not impress people any more than private ones, many of which are also excellent.

On the contrary, it seems that the public tends to feel vaguely suspicious about anything sponsored by the state or the government. They suspect that the truth is somewhat distorted, and that governmental authorities behave in an annoyingly persistent way.

About five or six years ago, Japanese diplomats, businessmen, journalists, etc., living in New York gathered at the Japanese consulate. "It is regrettable that Japan-U.S. relations have become as strained as they now appear to be. On every occasion the Americans demand that Japan open its markets. But actually, Japan has been opening its markets, albeit gradually, according to America's demands. I wonder if it is the lack of publicity or PR on the part of Japan concerning this gradual advance that is causing these strained relations," the Consul-General said at the beginning of the meeting. Those present were roughly divided between those who looked as if they disagreed with the Consul-General's opinion and those who seemed to agree.

Japanese businessmen tend to try to avoid being the first to speak under such circumstances. Japanese advertising may indeed be insufficient, but on the other hand, it might not be a question of PR at all. The only real solution perhaps is to promote market liberalization at a faster rate. But businessmen usually keep their mouths shut when they have a definite opinion.

Sure enough, a journalist was the first to offer a comment: "Advertising is useless. Pressure from the U.S. will continue until the markets are actually opened up. Rather than PR per se, an unequivocal attitude is what is required of Japan. For instance, Japan should say that such and such a field cannot be liberalized immediately because of such and such reasons, but that the plan is this and Japan will try to meet American expectations around such and such a date." I listened to him in silence but agreed with him completely.

The Private Sector's Effect on Japan's PR

It may not be 100 percent correct to say that in Japan the government has a stronger position vis-à-vis the private sector, and that in the U.S., the private sector has an advantage over the government. But I think there is very strong evidence showing tendencies in that direction.

I personally think that rather than the Japanese government paying money to do its own PR in other countries, it would be a hundred times more effective to let privately-owned Japanese organizations do the job.

A Japanese company called TDK built a local production plant in Georgia. As a token of appreciation toward its American neighbors, TDK made a video program about a day in the life of an ordinary Japanese high-school student, then distributed the videos in the community.

This film became quite popular among the Americans. The majority of the American public, who had only known about Japan through such TV specials as "Shogun" and Sho Kosugi's *ninja* movies were surprised to see that Japanese teenagers were no different from their own. They must have felt a sense of relief, and even some sympathy toward the Japanese.

A Finance Delegation from the U.S.

When I returned to Japan in December 1958, I received a call from President Tsunao Okumura (who became Chairman of Nomura Securities in 1959). With his usual southern Japanese accent, he said: "Now that you are back from the States, I want you to do something for me. I want to invite a delegation of financiers from the United States to see through their own eyes how Japan has rebuilt itself into a modern industrial nation after the war. As the old saying goes, 'Seeing is believing.' Would you write a letter to Mr. Eugene Black, the President of the World Bank, and ask him to recommend some names?"

So I wrote a letter to Eugene Black. He replied that he was not in a position to recommend people, but that I should consult Mr.

Woods, the Chairman of First Boston. We corresponded with Andrew Overby, who was working for Woods at the time. The year 1959 was spent preparing for the visit. The delegation finally landed in Japan in May 1960 through an invitation from the Japan Chamber of Commerce and Industry, the Federation of Economic Organizations, and Koshasai Hikiuke Kyokai (the Bond Underwriters Association of Japan), of which Mr. Okumura was the chairman.

The twenty members of the team included such people as Andrew Overby, Vice President of First Boston; J.A. Sheff, President of Kuhn Loeb; W.A. Forester, Vice President of Merrill Lynch; and F.B. Wild, President of Connecticut General Life Insurance.

After the plan was announced, the media hyped up the visit. Newspaper headlines read "Huge Capital to Come from Wall Street," "Okumura Lures the Dollars to Japan." Kabuto-cho, Japan's equivalent of Wall Street, praised the decision, seeing this as an opportunity to boost stock purchases.

The finance delegation stayed in Japan from May 8 to 18, 1960. The party traveled in limousines escorted by a police motorcade, a treatment usually reserved for state guests. The visit proved to be a great success. It stimulated exchange between the financial worlds in Japan and the U.S. Okumura's decision to invite this delegation was truly one of heroic proportions.

Sony's ADR

In June, 1960, the ADR manager of Morgan Guaranty Trust came to Japan. His mission was to persuade Japanese companies to issue ADRs. In reality, however, none of us knew precisely what an ADR, or American Depository Receipt, was. Some of us misunderstood the whole idea. This is how we believed it would work: Morgan would buy the stocks of 50 Japanese companies in large numbers with its own funds. Morgan would then sell the receipts, which are called ADRs, to Americans, keeping the stock certificates at the bank. One of the objectives of my trip to the U.S. was to understand how an ADR actually worked. Let me explain what I learned.

Mr. Smith in the U.S. buys 1,000 shares of Sony stock through Nomura Securities. He does not want to keep the stock certificates with him, so Nomura Securities sends the certificates to the Bank of Tokyo for safekeeping. The Bank of Tokyo telexes Morgan in New York, saying, "We're keeping Mr. Smith's Sony stock certificates. Would you issue a receipt in English and send it to Mr. Smith?" Morgan Stanley then sends a receipt—an ADR—to Mr. Smith.

An ADR itself is traded just like stock in the U.S. In our example, the ADR changed hands from Mr. Smith to Mr. Johnson, and then to Mr. Reagan. Mr. Reagan now wants the stock certificates, so he takes the ADR to Morgan. Morgan telexes the Bank of Tokyo, asking them to send the certificates to Mr. Reagan's account at Nomura Securities.

Now, going back to 1960, we suggested that Sony issue ADRs. We told them that they should integrate raising capital at market prices into their financial planning. But since the Japanese market was not ready for such an idea, Sony would try it in the U.S. Sony could then transfer only the face value into their capital account and distribute any excess capital raised to U.S. shareholders free of charge. This would keep Sony's stock price relatively high, and make the next stock issue easier.

Eventually, Sony offered an ADR with Nomura Securities and Smith Barney acting as managing underwriters. Sony issued 200,000 ADRs (2 million shares) for 3.5 million dollars (1.26 billion yen). The issuing price was $17.50 for one ADR, which consisted of 10 shares. We encountered all several difficulties on the way.

Our most difficult task was to explain the Japanese method of doing business to the satisfaction of the U.S. Securities and

Exchange Commission (SEC). We also had to change accounting methods to comply with the consolidation system used in the West. Akio Morita (Sony vice president at the time, currently chairman) found changing the accounting system frustrating and infuriating. Indeed, Morita admits in his *Made in Japan* that "the work [of issuing ADRs] may have been the hardest I ever had to do."

The registration statements became effective on June 1. When all was ready and the Sony ADR was to be released the next day, investor inquiries came to a sudden halt. After some investigation, we found that a news agency in Tokyo had reported on a possible coup d'état by the Self-Defense Forces in Japan. We protested to the news agency, and asked them to retract the story. After much wrangling, the ADR was finally put on the market. It was a great success—the buy orders were about thirty times higher than the number offered!

Sony's ADR issue was a landmark event in many ways. For one, it opened the way for a Japanese securities firm—in this case, Nomura—to become a lead manager (co-managing underwriter with Smith Barney). In those days, the market was run by Smith Barney, First Boston, Morgan Stanley, and other top Western companies. At a Smith Barney board meeting, I heard that some people insisted that Nomura should be given a lesser role. The idea was that if you let Nomura become lead manager, you would not be able to refuse other latecomers, such as Daiwa, Nikko, and Yamaichi. In the end, Ernest Schwartzenbach won out for Nomura.

Other Japanese companies did follow suit. The same year Sony issued the ADR, Sumitomo Metal Industries and Kawasaki Steel issued foreign currency bonds (common stock) for the first time since the end of World War II. Nippon Telegraph and Telephone Public Corporation (currently NTT) and the Japan Development Bank issued government-guaranteed bonds, while Mitsubishi Kasei made a private-bond offering. In the following year, Toshiba issued ADRs, and Shin Mitsubishi Heavy Industries (which changed to Mitsubishi Heavy Industries after a three-company integration in 1964) issued dollar-denominated convertible bonds.

Other Japanese Companies Offer Equities in the U.S.

Nomura Securities wanted to handle blue-chip companies such as Nippon Steel (formerly Yawata Steel and Fuji Steel), Toshiba, and Shin Mitsubishi Heavy Industries. In those days, however, big companies were overly conservative and bureaucratic. When a new suggestion was made, they would study it for a long time, but in the end, decide not to take the risk. Nomura, however, continued its campaign—as it firmly believed that all Japanese companies should raise capital in New York, the top market in the world.

One of our targets was Toshiba, a typically bureaucratic company. In October 1961, Toshiba merged with a company called Ishikawajima Shibaura Turbine, a joint venture of Toshiba and Ishikawajima-Harima Heavy Industries. After the merger, there was a lot of argument as to what should be done about the portion of the company's stock (50%) formerly owned by Ishikawajima-Harima Industries. At the suggestion of Nomura Securities, the stock was offered as ADRs in February 1962: 30 million shares totaling 9.3 million dollars.

This was a landmark event. The fact that a giant company like Toshiba offered its shares on the New York market, even though they were not newly issued stock, had a great impact in those days. Foundations and institutional investors in the U.S.—investment trusts and life insurance companies—made direct, large-scale investment in a Japanese firm for the first time. In December 1962, Toshiba raised capital on the New York market by issuing convertible dollar bonds worth a total of 20 million dollars.

Minoru Segawa, the top advisor to Nomura Securities, wrote in his book, *Watashi no showa shoken-shi* (My View of the History of Securities in the Showa Era): "If Sony's ADR issue was a single, Toshiba's was a home run! This was how I used to conclude my speech at meetings across the U.S., and it drew loud applause. At present, American investors are investing in Japanese companies through ADRs. My dream is to issue a JDR, or Japanese Depository Receipt, so that Japanese investors can own American securities."

Another leading Japanese company, Shin Mitsubishi Heavy Industries, offered convertible bonds in the U.S., worth a total of $10 million, in September 1962, three months ahead of Toshiba. This deal was also managed by Nomura Securities. It was the first convertible bond offering by a Japanese company on an overseas market since World War II.

Other companies followed, and issued convertible bonds and ADRs. The boom was brought on partly by the April 1963 scrapping of the limitations on the term of deferment for stocks owned by foreign investors. With Nomura's management, the Kansai Electric Power Company issued ADRs worth $21.8 million, and Sony made another ADR issue, worth $5.2 million. Mitsui & Co. issued $1.75 million worth of ADRs and $10 million worth of convertible bonds.

The Interest Equalization Tax

On July 18, 1963, (July 19 in Japan) the Kennedy administration announced an Interest Equalization Tax as one of the measures to improve the U.S. trade balance. The tax immediately stifled U.S. interest in foreign equity investment. The Interest Equalization Tax was a surcharge levied on American ownership of foreign securities. The initial rate of 15% was reduced gradually until it was finally repealed in January 1974.

At Kabuto-cho, a telex about the tax came in on July 16, but no one at Nomura Securities or the other Big Three securities firms knew what the Interest Equalization Tax was all about. Unfortunately, Tadashi Ishida, branch manager of Nomura New York, was out of town on summer vacation. The first day passed in sheer confusion, as nobody knew what to do. the Dow Jones Average slumped, falling 18 points (4.25%) on July 19, and 16 points on July 20.

Because of the tax, we found it virtually impossible to issue Japanese stocks in the U.S. A host of Japanese companies, such as Takeda Chemical Industries and Toyota Motor Corporation, had been planning to issue stock in the U.S. Nomura had been working hard to persuade Toyota. I got together with Akira Shimizu (former president of Nomura Securities International) and A. Mikuni (who now runs a rating agency) at a Japanese inn in Toyohashi city, Aichi prefecture. We visited Toyota every day for a week to draft a prospectus. We introduced Price Waterhouse to Toyota for an audit. Taizo Ishida, chairman of Toyota Motor Company, had set the condition that the firm could not audit for Nissan Motors, their major rival. Price Waterhouse agreed. But the whole project went up in smoke, as the Interest Equalization Tax ruined all our efforts. As you may be aware, to this day Toyota has not raised capital overseas. It may have been the first and last opportunity for Toyota.

The world's financial center shifted to Europe. In March 1964, Nomura opened its first business office in London. The office was headed by Keisuke Egashira. The London office was upgraded to a branch office in 1970.

Many years later, Tsunao Okumura (President at the time) told me there was an argument over whether they should send me or Egashira to London. In the end, they decided on Egashira because he was "a refined, true gentleman, who doesn't get drunk and yell." Since then, Egashira has become "Mr. Britain," and I am "Mr. America" in the minds of Nomura's employees.

On Being Promoted to New York Branch Manager

In July 1968, Nomura promoted me to Deputy Chief of the Foreign Affairs Department at Nomura's head office. Soon after, I was sent to New York, where I was to serve as branch manager; I stayed there for seven years. But Nomura Securities International, Inc. was established in September 1969, so I was the last New York branch manager. I was still young—37.

The challenge for us at the time was to incorporate Japanese stocks into American investment trusts. There were some European funds that specialized mainly in Japanese stocks: for instance, the Nippon Fund by Vickers Da Costa in Britain. In the U.S., the Japan Fund was the only fund which incorporated Japanese stocks. By 1969, American fund companies such as Keystone and Dreyfus had bought a massive amount of Japanese stocks. That meant U.S. fund companies with huge amounts of capital had started to buy Japanese stocks just as they would buy American stocks. The Japanese stock market was, at last, on its way to becoming truly international.

Nomura's New York branch was turned into a local corporation. By the mid-sixties, Japanese companies like Hitachi and Toshiba were competing shoulder to shoulder with General Electric. The fund companies wanted to know how the Japanese companies were doing in comparison with GE. They suggested that if we became a member of the Boston Stock Exchange, they could place orders to the Boston Stock Exchange through us. The Boston Stock Exchange had opened its doors to foreign companies in 1968, well ahead of the New York Stock Exchange in 1977, where I became a member in 1981.

To be eligible for joining the Boston Stock Exchange, the company had to be a local corporation. Also, the Boston Stock Exchange membership is individual, which means that I, as the representative, had to pass a written examination and have a physical check-up. For the written exam, I reviewed bookkeeping and accounting for the first time in many years. The physical check-up is required to guard against cardiac arrest because trading strains your heart.

On November 24, 1969, I received a notice saying I had passed the exam. I was asked to go to the Boston Stock Exchange. When I entered the BSE, about 20 reporters were there with their cameras. Wondering if a VIP was coming to the exchange, I entered the director's room. The director said: "Congratulations. We are the oldest stock exchange in the nation. And you are the first member from the Orient." The reporters' cameras flashed.

A thick, leather-bound constitution lay on the table. I opened it and saw the names of all the members, from the very first signature signed in 1700 with a feather pen. The yellowed pages conveyed its age. In a flash of inspiration, I signed the book in *kanji* characters to show my Japanese identity. TV reporters were delighted to film the event.

In September 1969, Nomura's New York, Los Angeles, and Honolulu branches had been integrated to form Nomura Securities International (NSI). Operations began in November 1969. The first president of NSI was Yukio Aida, who also served as Managing Director of the Nomura head office (later chairman of Nomura Securities Co., Ltd.). I was the Vice President and de facto commander-in-chief of NSI. The New York head office started out with ten employees, and the Los Angeles and Honolulu offices had five employees each.

Meanwhile, the Japanese financial market was slowly opening its doors to the outside world. By 1965, it was clear to the Japanese government that Japan's trade surplus was here to stay, and it launched measures to liberalize foreign investment. In February 1970, the government approved the inclusion of foreign securities in domestic investment trusts. Under an eight-point plan announced in July 1971, Japanese individual investors were now free to invest in stocks and bonds listed on the stock exchanges of OECD member nations.

On June 29, 1971, my fourth child and first son was born in New York. That event must have given me strength and inspiration, because on June 30, I called the *New York Times* and said, "From tomorrow, Japanese investors will be able to buy American stocks. We will have orders coming in from Tokyo. If you want to get a picture of this historic moment, you should come tomorrow morning at 7:40 a.m." Congratulatory orders came in through the ticker tape. The *New York Times* carried a big photo of me handling the orders.

For Japan, it marked a major turning point, from an import-oriented era—or as Nomura's catch-phrase puts it: the era when "money flowed into the Japanese market"—to an export-oriented era. Yet, individual investors in Japan were not yet ready to buy American or British stocks in large quantities. Securities houses, therefore, persuaded them to invest, say, 5% of their funds in foreign equities.

Another event rocked the industry immediately after the government liberalized foreign investment. At 9 p.m. on Sunday, August 15, 1971 (10 a.m. on Monday, August 16 in Japan)—I will never forget this date—President Nixon announced on TV a 10% import surcharge and the elimination of the gold standard. The announcement plunged the international financial market into shock, and seriously dampened Japanese investors' enthusiasm for foreign securities investment.

The Nikkei–Dow Jones Stock Average plummeted 210 points, the largest drop ever. In four days, the Nikkei average fell 17%. The Japanese economy—and financial authorities in particular—panicked. The picture, however, was completely different in New York. The Dow Jones Industrial Average jumped by 32.93, the largest gain in history. In addition, on August 28, the market shifted to a floating rate system, ending the exchange rate of 360 to a dollar that had been in place since April 1949.

During this crisis, I was deeply impressed by the work of Yusuke Kashiwagi (Finance Ministry advisor at the time, later

Chairman of the Bank of Tokyo). He worked an extra-tight schedule, flying to the U.S. every week to solve various problems.

In December 1971, the Smithsonian Agreement revived a fixed exchange rate of $1=¥308, but it did not last long. In February 1972, the floating rate system was back in place.

The Japanese government unveiled a seven-point economic plan in May 1972. Under that plan, the government lifted all restrictions on foreign securities investment by Japanese residents.

One more event cast a cloud over that time. In March 1973, Naomichi Toyama, President of Nikko Securities, was killed in a plane crash on his way back from Majorca, Spain. He was 47. I used to encounter Nikko Securities men, headed by "Nao-chan," at various gatherings. He was my competitor, but I was close to him personally. In New York, we often went out to dinner. Toyama was an attractive, international-minded person, and his death was a great loss both to the securities industry and to me personally.

On Becoming an Honorary Citizen of New York

The City Club of New York is organized by dyed-in-the-wool New Yorkers. It is a private club, comprised of people from many different occupations, and it oversees and supports the city's administration. Once a year, the City Club honors Americans who have contributed greatly to the City of New York. The black-tie award ceremony is held in the Waldorf Astoria ballroom, which can hold more than 3,000 people.

In 1973, the City Club of New York decided to award honors to some foreign residents. Eight people were named from many different areas. They included an eye doctor from Spain who had been treating New Yorkers for thirty years; a star Canadian player with the Rangers; and two Japanese, Soichi Kawazoe, Vice President of Nissan Motors U.S., and myself.

I received the award for handling the first Japanese securities investment on Wall Street and stimulating the New York market. The *New York Times* had carried my picture, as I mentioned earlier, which must have singled me out among other Japanese.

Soichi Kawazoe, of course, sold Nissan cars. He had also set up a big camp in New Jersey, and invited children from low-income families to come there for their summer vacation. His generous efforts in this area earned him the award. Low-income families, in many cases, do not have the resources to send their children to camps. Nissan's Kawazoe invited hundreds of low-income kids, most of them black, to his New Jersey camp.

GM, the John Wayne of Stocks

In November 1974, the year after the first oil crisis, foreign securities were listed on the Tokyo Stock Exchange for the first time. Our dreams had reached fruition. As I mentioned earlier, foreign investment by individual Japanese investors was liberalized on July 1, 1971. It was now our task to lure foreign securities to the Tokyo market and establish them in Japan. Nomura Securities approached General Motors and some other companies. Nikko, Daiwa, and Yamaichi Securities were also contacting leading American firms. Nomura told them: "In the future, Tokyo will become one of the big three capital markets in the world. A listing on the Tokyo Stock Exchange will generate great publicity."

However, trading was not profitable for some of the foreign companies that listed on the TSE. I think the time was not yet ripe, unlike today, when more than 60 foreign companies are listed on the TSE. And that number will increase to over 100 companies before the end of this year.

Nomura tried many things. We asked Ichiro Hattori of Daini Seikosha Company Limited (President of Seiko, Seiko Epson Corporation, and Seiko Instruments, Inc.) to purchase General Motors stock and attend the stockholders' meeting in Detroit, Michigan. Mr. and Mrs. Hattori met the GM President there. This was done to publicize the presence of a Japanese GM stockholder.

I thought the best way to impress the American public was for a Japanese company to buy GM stock. Automobiles symbolize America. GM, the maker of the Cadillac, is the John Wayne of all stocks—powerful and strong. We had hoped this would encourage U.S. investors to buy Japanese stocks such as Toyota. American holders of Japanese stocks would be concerned about the performance of Toyota, and Japanese stockholders would care about GM's moves. I believed that two-way increased private stock investment in the other country—between Japan and the U.S.—would help alleviate the trade conflict between the two countries. This, in my opinion, is the true bond that ties capitalistic and free trade economies.

May Day on Wall Street

I assumed the post of President of Nomura Securities International in 1972. In December 1974, I was appointed Director of the Nomura head office. In early 1975, some people in Washington brought up the argument that stock commissions should be deregulated, just like all other commissions. And on May 1, 1975, the deregulation took effect.

May 1, 1975, was "May Day," the landmark day on which fixed brokerage comissions were abolished in the U.S. The deregulation plunged the securities industry into a maelstrom. The London Securities Exchange carried out a large-scale systematic reform. In the case of the 1975 "May Day" in the U.S., someone started to use the word about two months after the deregulation came into effect. It indeed took place on the first day of May—"May Day." Also, the word "May Day" is used as a call for help, like S.O.S. The word May Day originally comes from "M' aidez" in French, which means "help me." It is the international call for help, used by a ship or aircraft in distress. So, the U.S. stock market has given the phrase a double meaning implying that the market was in trouble.

As I mentioned earlier, Nomura Securities International became a member of the Boston Stock Exchange in 1969. The Boston Stock Exchange membership has been open to institutional investors as well as to non-American companies (and their subsidiaries). With the development of telecommunications networks, stock orders have tended to converge on the New York Stock Exchange. The Boston Stock Exchange opened its doors to stem the tide, to lure orders back to Boston. Many companies took advantage of the institutional membership. It was now possible, say, for Metropolitan Life Insurance to make its brokerage subsidiary a member of the Boston Stock Exchange, and to place orders through that subsidiary. By doing it this way, the commissions paid would stay inside the corporate group, and the volume traded at the Boston Stock Exchange would increase.

The New York Stock Exchange, however, has never allowed institutional investor membership, and that has remained unchanged to this day. If it did, institutional investors such as life insurance, pension, and investment trust companies would place orders through their subsidiary securities companies. This would then rob conventional securities firms of the bulk of orders. That was one of the reasons behind the brokerage commission deregulation.

The impact of deregulation was profound. In the first stage, commissions for small-lot orders—mainly by individual investors—went up because of "incurring costs." Commissions for institutional investors plunged to about one third the pre-deregulation level. Then, the emergence of discount brokers set off "dumping," lowering the commissions for small-lot orders. Unlike a full-service broker, which has a research department and offers advice on investment, the discount broker simply executes clients' orders. Because of their low overhead, discount brokers are able to charge lower commissions than full-service brokers. In any event, the deregulation triggered a reorganization of the U.S. securities industry.

Before "May Day," mergers and acquisitions were active and the number of securities houses was on the decline. After "May Day," new entrants into the market made the situation more fluid. Conventional securities companies turned away from the commission-generating business to trading (mainly bonds) for their primary source of income.

Once again, mergers flourished. Retail houses that targeted individual investors were generally weak on research, with the exception of some like Merrill Lynch. By contrast, service brokers had good research departments, but they were suffering from a commission-price war. Mutually advantageous mergers between these two types of companies occurred, such as the acquisition of Harris Upham by Smith Barney in 1976.

New York Stock Exchange Membership

Membership in the New York Stock Exchange had long been the dream of Minoru Segawa. In 1977, Chairman Segawa was informed by Donald Regan, then Chairman of Merrill Lunch, that the New York Stock Exchange would open its membership to non-American companies. Segawa replied that Nomura would be delighted to join the club.

The New York Stock Exchange opened its membership to non-American firms in 1977. As in the case of Boston, the membership is individual, even if the entrance fees are paid by the company. To join the club, a representative from the company has to pass a skills-and-knowledge test. I was elected to take the test again, this time for Nomura's entrance into the New York Stock Exchange membership. But I was confident, since it would be my second test after the one for the Boston Stock Exchange. I wanted to become the first Japanese member, as I knew other Japanese companies were bound to join the Exchange sooner or later.

I had one reservation. I was concerned about the U.S. reaction: would it encourage U.S. securities firms to demand membership on the Tokyo Stock Exchange? In those days, the Tokyo Stock Exchange was no match for the New York Stock Exchange. You could compare American securities firms to professional baseball teams, and their Japanese counterparts to minor league teams. Japanese securities were playing sandlot baseball inside Japan, and now they want to play at Yankee Stadium. Why shouldn't U.S. securities firms be allowed to play at Japan's Korakuen Stadium? I feared that the Ministry of Finance and the securities companies in Japan might say, "All Nomura has done is put us all in hot water. Nomura should have minded its own business."

So to avoid this kind of reaction, I visited the Securities Companies Division of the Securities Bureau of Japan's Ministry of Finance, and told them that I wanted to join the New York Stock Exchange. I asked them unofficially if they would approve this. To my surprise, the Ministry replied "yes" in just one week. I was, and still am, truly grateful for the Ministry's decision.

On July 26, 1981—the day I joined the New York Stock Exchange—TV cameras surrounded me at the Stock Exchange. In my speech, I said, "When I became a member of the New York Stock Exchange, the first thing I did was to buy General Motors' stock because GM is the John Wayne of the U.S. securities market."

Unexpected, the American employees of NSI came up to the President's office to say, "Congratulations!" They said they were proud to be working for Nomura, which was now a member firm. Becoming a member helped boost employee morale and made me realize that a member firm was in a different league altogether from non-member firms.

Membership status, just like the primary dealer status that we obtained later, enhances a company's credit. Also, member firms are subject to surprise audits. These are the reasons why a member firm is preferred over a non-member firm as a business partner, even if all other conditions are the same. It gives a firm's name substantial prestige to write "Member — New York Stock Exchange" under the company sign and on its letterhead.

The securities industry is a kind of guild, and you have to join the guild to do business. Kabuto-cho in Japan, dubbed the "island," is a rather closed society. Wall Street and the City in London, too, have a similar nature. I guess securities industries are destined to be restrictive. There is this expression: "My word is my bond." When, for instance, someone wants to buy 1 billion units of interest-bearing government bonds, and you say, "O.K. It's sold," the deal is done. Even if the interest rate changes before the bonds are handed over, and you know you are going to incur a huge loss, you cannot cancel the deal. You have to keep your word. The industry has relied heavily on trust, and I suppose that that is one of the reasons why they do not admit outsiders freely.

I believe this is why Chairman Segawa insisted on our becoming a member of the New York Stock Exchange. Since becoming a member, I have tried as much as possible to take part in various meetings. After becoming a member, I felt that I was allowed into the living room, rather than saying hello on the doorstep. And, indeed, such informal talks and comments proved to be truly important.

Primary Dealer Status

The waves of change for deregulation and internationalization were sweeping the financial markets in the U.S., Japan, and Europe. The U.S.-Japan Yen-Dollar Committee meeting was held in May 1984. In June 1985, nine foreign banks in Japan received authorization from the Ministry of Finance to enter the trust banking industry. In December 1985, six foreign securities companies were allowed, for the first time, to become members of the Tokyo Stock Exchange. The Group of Five reached the Plaza Accord in New York in September 1985. The agreement set the stage for the appreciation of the yen.

The U.S. securities market was shaken by frequent stock cornering and takeover bids. Junk bonds made their appearance around 1982, and M & A (mergers and acquisitions) picked up speed. The boom slowed down some after the Ivan Boesky insider trading scandal of 1986. In Japan, the stock market moved toward expansion and diversification using futures and options trading on both bonds and stock indices.

The U.S. and Japan finally entered an era of low interest rates. In early 1987, the New York Dow Jones Average cleared 2,000, while the TSE Stock Average exceeded 20,000.

My last job in New York was to apply to the New York Federal Reserve to become a primary dealer in U.S. government securities. Our application was approved in December 1986. At present, a group of 40 leading firms enjoy primary dealer status. Primary dealers conduct business directly with the Federal Reserve in open-market operations.

Primary dealer status entails heavy obligations. Primary dealers are committed to making markets in all treasury issues. They must meet minimum levels of trading in Treasury auctions, even if it means buying Treasury bonds at a loss. The Fed supplies exclusive information to primary dealers on hot-lines in exchange for their commitment to buy and sell even in times of trouble.

The benefits of such status include substantial prestige. Primary dealers are the five-star holders of the securities industry. When state governments order Treasury bonds for pension and fund management, they choose a primary dealer over a non-primary dealer in otherwise equal conditions.

As a matter of fact, we were not very interested in primary dealer status in the beginning when our foremost concern was to sell Japanese stocks in the U.S. But as we started to import U.S. government bonds to Japan, it was evident that we had to obtain primary dealer status. The path to primary dealership status was rocky one. In March 1985, we started by writing letters to all primary dealers—36 at the time—asking them to support us in becoming a primary dealer. We encountered three kinds of responses. We wrote a letter of thanks to those who supported us. For those requesting us to come and explain, we did so. We also visited the primary dealers who were opposed to our primary dealership in order to determine why they were opposed.

We had a hard time convincing the Americans, who tend to have a reciprocal way of thinking. They would ask us, "If we let you in, will we be able to become a primary dealer in Japan?" But there is no status that corresponds to primary dealership status in Japan.

From January 1986, we began to submit daily reports to the New York Fed and were audited on our Treasury bond trading, which was then followed by a financial audit. By then, we were fairly certain the Fed would grant us primary dealership.

However, there was one more incident along the way. U.S. congressman Charles Schumer, who had visited Japan wrote to the President of the New York Fed, arguing against granting primary dealership to a Japanese securities firm. He said, "The Japanese market is still closed. Even Salomon Brothers, the largest U.S. securities company, has not been allowed to become a member of the Tokyo Stock Exchange."

I was relieved when the Fed informed us on December 11,

1986, that they would grant us primary dealership status. I had been afraid that we would have to wait until another year.

I had stayed in the U.S. on and off for 16 years starting in 1956, which is half the time I worked for Nomura. It is unusual, even for the "internationalists" of Nomura, to spend so long in one country. Usually, they spend their time in different countries, say five years in London, three years in Hong Kong and five years in New York.

During my stay in New York, I had traveled to Japan many times on business. But this time (January 1987), it felt different, since I was going back to stay in, and not just travel to, Japan. I will certainly often fly from Tokyo to New York on business. But staying in New York on a business trip will never be the same as staying there on assignment.

3

Memories of New York

The Nobel Prize vs. Adherence to a Standard

I do not remember for sure if the principal had a sword on his hip. I know he was in a military uniform. The loudspeaker was making screeching noises and I could not hear what was being said by the Emperor. "The war is over," the principal cried. His face was red with excitement.

On August 15, 1945, all the students were standing in lines at attention in the schoolyard. Forty years later, as I stand in the same schoolyard, the memory of the shock of the defeat that ruined our school life comes back to me as if it were only yesterday. I visited my school the other day for the first time in forty years. I was to give a speech at its 89th anniversary ceremony. One thousand male students were waiting quietly in the gymnasium for my arrival. "Rise," "Bow," "Be seated." The young men in their black school uniforms did exactly as they were told, like clockwork toys.

The strong summer sun is shining on the fountain in the center of the square. A graduation ceremony is about to start at the Concert Hall of Lincoln Center in New York. The fifteen hundred seats are almost all filled. In America, at a graduation ceremony, graduating students wear a gown and square cap just like the one on the statue of Shigenobu Okuma* at Waseda University. My

* Shigenobu Okuma: the founder of Waseda University

second oldest daughter, Haruko, is graduating from the School of Visual Arts. About 500 graduating students, standing near the stage, are dressed in individual styles and colors, as if they are protesting against the unsophisticated conventional caps and gowns.

The university president hands out a rolled diploma to each student. Each time a student steps up to the stage, cheers and applause rise from the audience, and they seem louder when a blonde girl goes up. One Oriental student with a pencil appearing to protrude from his head waltzes to the stage. He has the air of demonstrating that he has studied hard to obtain this piece of paper. When a female student holding a baby in her hands goes up and the President hands out two diplomas, there is a stir in the audience. Some of the students kiss the president. Some of them embrace him and even dance with him on the stage. It is a hopelessly disorderly and gay graduation—and a sight you would never see in Japan. Haruko later told me that the real diplomas were given to the students in the President's office after the graduation. She showed me the rolled paper, and it said "Congratulations!" No wonder the President gave one to a little baby without hesitation.

In one week I had seen an extreme contrast between order and disorder, between control and liberty, and it made me reflect. One educational system emphasizes the freedom and development of each child's individuality, and the other is a uniform education that regiments children. It is not necessarily true that the former is the American system and the latter the Japanese system. And even if it is so, I honestly do not know which is better.

Until 1966, Japan was considered to be one of the underdeveloped countries among the World Bank members. On July 15, 1991, Japan finally paid off the loan it had received from the World Bank for constructing Japan's major highway system, Tomei Highway. Japan is now feared by the world as an economic superpower, but until recently Japan still had debts to the World Bank. Japan's rapid economic growth surprised the world, like an unremarkable student making a sudden leap to the top of the class. The economic growth was achieved by the diligent and industrious work of each and every one of the citizens. And the uniform education which aimed to raise the overall level of students was perhaps the factor behind the economic success.

There was an American prodigy who entered MIT at the age of 13 and graduated at 17 with a Ph.D. in mathematics. I wonder if, when he is thrown into society at large, he will be able to get along. It will be difficult for him, for although he may be a genius in mathematics, he doesn't know about anything else. This sort of thing could never happen in Japan, where the education system requires you to do well in all subjects in order to pass a university entrance examination. However, a Nobel Prize genius like Dr. Susumu Tonegawa* can be produced only in an American education environment.

In America, many things you see, automobiles, electrical appliances, cameras, etc., are made in Japan. Because things made in Japan are of good quality, even the most penny-pinching Americans buy Japanese products. Good quality is based on total quality control. If top priority is given to the improvement of productivity, Japanese uniform education will be the winner.

"Do you want me to tell you the truth?" Tom, my former classmate from University of Pennsylvania gave me a shock.

"If a European businessman offered a product of the same quality as the Japanese at the same kind of price, I would definitely buy the European one."

"But, why?" I asked, and he replied, "Japanese businessmen talk about nothing but business, whereas British businessmen can

* Dr. Susumu Tonegawa: Nobel Prize winner for medicine for 1987

talk about Shakespeare, and French businessmen will never run out of topics on art or food." Unfortunately, Japanese businessmen are not considered to be very interesting. One of the reasons is the language barrier. But the Japanese educational system, which stresses adherence to a standard and makes students lose enthusiasm once they enter universities—after having gone through the ordeal of entrance examination—is also to blame. The shallow and superficial knowlede gained in preparing for examinations is not enough to compete with first-class European and American businessmen. The day when emphasis is placed not only on the quality of the products, but also on that of the people who handle the products, will, hopefully, come before too long.

The Bells of Trinity Church

Do not be discouraged if the New York taxi drivers do not understand your English, for nearly half of them are foreigners, too. I said to a taxi driver, "To Wall Street," over and over again. I was quite annoyed, but I was finally able to make myself understood after repeating the words, patiently. It was Monday, August 6. There were occasional heavy showers, but the sun came out after a while, though it was somewhat muggy. I did not have any special business to attend to. I simply wondered how my friends on Wall Street were doing since the Iraqi invasion of Kuwait. It was not that I had been asked by anyone. I wanted to see them so badly that as soon as I arrived at La Guardia Airport from Washington, I got in a taxi and the words "To Wall Street" jumped out of my mouth.

The big clock of Trinity Church showed exactly two o'clock. I entered the stock exchange building at 20 Broad Street. Spectators are supposed to enter from there to observe the New York stock exchange. A tall and heavily-built man who looked like a wrestler came toward me. "*Kippu, wari, wari,*" he muttered in unintelligible Japanese. I did not have the patience to deal with his effort to speak Japanese. I wanted to get in to the session without a moment's delay. "I would like to get in immediately. What should I do?" I asked him in English. He stubbornly kept talking to me in Japanese. I had no alternative but to try to figure out what he was saying. And I got it! He was saying *"kippu ga owatta"* (admission tickets are all finished) and so I could not go in. I had no choice but to go around to the entrance for the members of the exchange. I was a member myself until three years ago, and that was the entrance I went through many times before with a badge on my chest. I am a non-member now and I no longer own a badge, so I cannot enter through there. Then I remembered Peter, a floor man [boardman]. I asked for Peter and he appeared in less than five minutes. He looked rather pale. I was given a visitor's badge and went in with Peter. The Dow Index was down 75 points. The floor was awfully quiet. On the Black Monday of October 19, 1987, the floor was in a tumult. The trading volume was six hundred million shares and the Dow Index fell by 508. "It is not normal that the stock is so high," "It won't be surprising if it declines when some special factors emerge somewhere." Into such an atmosphere flew the bad news from the Middle East. And that was why the stock exchange was so quiet, as if they thought there was no point in getting agitated. (This slump is feminine compared to that of Black Monday, which was a masculine slump. That is, men raise their hands when in a fit of rage, whereas women become calm and even smile when truly angered. It is a frightening phenomenon.)

Peter is a specialist trader of Sony shares. Specialist is equivalent to *saitori* (broker) on the Tokyo stock exchange. The only difference is that specialists not only match buying and selling from the floor brokers of the member brokerage firms, but also have to buy when there is only selling and no buying, and sell when there is only buying and no selling. Needless to say, the stock price is established only when there is both selling and buying. The most important responsibility of the specialists is to establish the price. The oblong notebook Peter carries is called an "*ita*" (board) on the Tokyo stock exchange. The left-hand page is for selling and the right-hand for buying. Floor brokers who receive instructions from their head offices to buy or sell Sony shares gather at Peter's post. Then Peter matches the selling and buying looking at the *ita*.

I was afraid I was chatting with Peter too long, but no one came to him. "Business seems to be slow, doesn't it?" "Yes, things are different now. If they want to buy Sony shares they go to the Tokyo Stock Exchange. It is extremely slow," said Eugene, who was sitting beside Peter and smiling, which was rather inappropriate for a time like this. Eugene is a rather small, bearded, and really good-natured man. But even he had a stern look on his face on Black Monday.

Peter began to explain, "If the oil price goes up now, there will be inflation in the American economy which is already showing such a tendency. If Japanese life insurance companies and other institutional investors buy American government bonds, the U.S. Government will have no choice but to raise the interest rate on bonds." He then concluded by saying "After all, the market hates uncertainties."

I said, "Thank you," and was going to leave, when Eugene came to me and whispered into my ear, "Actually, our company is on the market. We don't know yet who's going to buy it, so I haven't been able to take a summer holiday yet." Eugene, who is usually cheerful, looked a little despondent.

I came to the exit of the stock exchange to find it pouring rain outside. Since the buildings in the neighborhood didn't offer any shelter from rain, some ten people were hanging around at the entrance. Stepping out into the downpour, I started walking eastward on Wall Street. It was raining so fiercely I was instantly drenched to the skin. My newly purchased Brooks Brothers navy suit, tie with navy polka dots on gold, and my new Churchill black shoes were all soaked with rain.

I have a habit of hurting myself by banging my head against a wall when I have seen or done something I should have not. Since I was wet already, why should I not make myself wet through and through. I felt the sadistic pleasure. The bells of Trinity Church tolled. It was two-thirty in the afternoon.

My Daughter's Wedding

On a day in May 1985, the room of Waseda University's Wandervogel Club was dark, filthy and smelly. "It's your alma mater. Let's go and visit Akiko," my wife was pressuring me, and we went to see our eldest daughter Akiko soon after the commencement.

My wife, who had taken it for granted that Akiko would choose Keio University, her alma mater, over fierce rival Waseda, was very upset to discover the contrary, and was convinced that I must have schemed something. According to her, Waseda was to blame for Akiko's devoting herself to Wandervogel activities, and neglecting her academic curriculum, for which I was to blame because I had influenced Akiko to choose Waseda. I can understand my wife's feelings because she is so proud of herself for being one of the first to graduate from Keio Women's High School, and is such an ardent admirer of Keio that she included in the conditions for our marriage that I should call the baseball match between the two universities Keiso-sen (Keio-Waseda) rather than Sokei-sen (Waseda-Keio) thereafter.

There is no way to find out if Akiko could have been happier if she had chosen Keio, or if she became dissatisfied because she was at Waseda. But it is quite understandable that Akiko, who had spent six years of primary school and three years of high school in America, and who had believed that she would continue her education in America, became disillusioned when she saw the hopelessly unenthusiastic students of Waseda, which made her seek refuge in the Wandervogel Club.

I was living in New York on my own at that time. Whenever I went home to Tokyo, which happened four or five times a year, my wife complained to me of the children's conduct. I dutifully listened to her, because I felt guilty at not being there for the children most of the time. I suppose that the role I was playing was an easy one, because I only occasionally saw them and was not there to share their joys and sorrows. Perhaps the role my wife had to play was a much harder one, scolding the children day after day.

Akiko led my wife and me to the Wandervogel room. Instantly I saw something white move. It turned out to be a big man in a white shirt. The man said "I am Yoneyama," and bowed. Since it was almost lunch time, we, including the big man, went to the Sancho-an restaurant. The restaurant, in the neighborhood of Waseda, is a well-known noodle shop with a history, but I do not remember the details. I used to go there very often about 40 years ago as a student, but it has changed a lot since then, having been renovated. The ground floor was full, so we went upstairs, and ordered for the big man a large bowl of noodles with tempura. He finished it in no time, and I ordered *katsudon* (deep fried pork cutlet on rice) for him.

"Are you all right for time?" Akiko looked at him concernedly. "Is anything the matter?" I asked, and he said calmly, "I have an examination at 1:30." My watch said 1:25. "You must hurry then," I said to him. He said "Yes," but did not move until he finished the last grain of rice in his bowl. "I enjoyed it very, very much"—so saying he stood up and went down the stairs, holding a thick book under his arm. The stairs creaked beneath his feet.

On December 10, 1991, Akiko called me at work from Tokyo. I sometimes call her, but she hardly ever calls me, so I wondered if something was wrong.

"Dad, I am thinking of getting married before the end of the year."

"To whom?"

"To Yone-san, who else? Next year is the year of the monkey (*saru* in Japanese) and it is bad luck to marry then. (*Saru* also means to leave.) Will you approve of my marriage to him?"

They had been seeing each other for six years, and I liked him from the first meeting. So I said "Yes, it's OK with me."

"I am so glad you said that." Akiko's voice at the other end of the line sounded cheerful. Her mother had hung up on her saying, "Before the end of the year?! That's absurd! There's less than three weeks left. There isn't enough time for proper preparation." Oh well, it seems as if I played the kind role again.

It is December 28, 1991, at one o'clock in the afternoon, and we are at Hikawa Shrine in Koenji, Tokyo. The shrine retains something reminiscent of a village shrine. Akiko chose this shrine for her wedding because I was born next to it. My deceased mother used to take me there on every special occasion—when I started high school and university, before I left for America to study. To maintain the tradition, my wife used to take our children to the shrine for every event that took place in the Terasawa family.

Akiko was standing gracefully to be photographed, wearing an immaculate white kimono and heavy-looking wig.

"Perhaps you don't remember, but that's the kimono I wore at our wedding," my wife said. Not having recognized it, I looked at the kimono again more closely.

"It is natural that you don't remember because you were so nervous," my mother-in-law defended me.

It was a very small wedding with only twenty guests, ten from each family. The ceremony proceeded in the small shrine. The priest, wearing a black headdress, made a deep bow before the altar as he chanted the long Shinto prayers.

Outside the lattice screen before the shrine, a middle-aged woman, dressed in jeans and sweater, threw money into the offertory chest, rang the bells, and prayed with her hands clasped.

When the ceremony was over we went outside. Yoneyama's *haori* (half coat) and *hakama* (divided skirt for man's formal wear) suited the tall and sturdily-built groom.

"Congratulations," I said to him and shook his hand. "Please take good care of Akiko."

"I will," he held my hand firmly.

The rain had stopped, and the snow which had fallen the previous day was mostly gone. The cold air felt very pleasant.

"Intestiognomy"

Even if I think that someone has gained weight since I last saw them, I will never say so to the person concerned, because I do not want to offend them. But, surprisingly, many people do not hesitate to say such things to one's face as "you have put on quite a bit of weight" or "you have developed a pot belly." I suppose not everyone in the world possesses as delicate a sensibility as I do. Those cruel words will hurt the person's feelings, like being touched on a sore spot, because they are already annoyed by their gain in weight.

A woman I used to know as a student may take the precautionary measure before our first meeting after 30 years of phoning me beforehand to say "I have gained so much weight. Don't be surprised when you see me." And I respond, "I am not presentable either. My hair has turned grey." I try thus to make her feel better, but find it difficult to imagine that she, who used to look so delicate and slender, has changed, and I wonder if it would be better if I did not see her now, so that I can keep the image of her that I have always had.

Somehow Americans do not say things to offend people. When I see my old acquaintances after some years, they always say "You look very well." That cannot be true. I have deninitely gained weight, and my hair has turned grey. I know they are only flattering me, but it does not make me feel uncomfortable.

I try to say "You look well" before they say it to me, unless they obviously look worn out, after a heart attack or some other serious illness, in which case I remain silent. Conversely speaking, when Americans do not say anything to me, I feel I must look exhausted.

It is not going to change the world whether you are fat or thin, and gentlemen should not comment on others' physical appearances, nor should you let others' comments bother you. I can very well understand the feeling of the writer who once said that he was disgusted with his own pettiness at being emotionally affected by the slight change in his weight. Not only do you not look nice when you gain weight, but your blood pressure and cholesterol level rise, your bodily functions begin to fail, and you will be scolded by your doctor. It may not be so bad while your doctors still scold you, but they may give up on you in the course of time, and that is terrifying.

I very much realize that I am being terribly selfish, but sometimes I seriously wish I were dead, although I do not want to become ill. I want to stay healthy. I am not afraid of death, but I am afraid of illness. No, the truth is that I am also afraid of death. And I know I cannot kill myself. I am only indulging myself in the sweet imagination that death will free me from all pains and problems.

People stay alive for various reasons such as the masculine feeling that they cannot die before they accomplish certain things, or the heroic sense of obligation that without them certain persons would not be able to get by, or the desire to live because they find that life is a joy. But only God knows when death will visit you. Since you cannot plan to meet your death in a noble way, for you do not know when you will die, ordinary people live to the best of their ability, wishing to live nobly at least.

I picked up a taxi next to Central Park, hurried the driver to get to La Guardia Airport, and just made a six o'clock flight to Washington. I was walking along the aisle of the plane when a man pulled my jacket. It was Dr. Hiromitsu Shinya. The seat next to his was empty so I sat down there. Dr. Shinya is my doctor who checks my digestive organs with an endoscope once a year. He was going to Washington to give a speech at a medical conference, and was to return to New York on the nine o'clock flight. He is not much younger than I, because he was born in 1935, but with his black hair and healthy complexion, he looks as if he is in his mid-40s.

Dr. Shintani coined a word in Japanese for which the nearest English equivalent would be "intestiognomy" to describe the physical shape and size of intestines. He learned, by looking with an endoscope at the intestines of some 50 patients every day, that every intestine has a different appearance, just like the differences of physiognomies. There are fine-featured intestines and abhorrent-looking intestines. How your intestines look entirely depends on what you eat. You will have good intestinal features if you eat brown rice, organic vegetables, and well-balanced meals in various combinations. Dr. Shinya was going to attend a dinner party, but he had in his bag some rice balls made with brown rice that his wife had prepared for him.

When we parted, I thought I would follow his example, but I know that I do not have a strong enough will to keep to it. It is about time for another endoscopy. I wonder how my intestines look.

Five More Days to Live

Henry Dorman is a dandy. He lives in New York on Fifth Avenue and leaves for work at six-thirty every morning. I used to leave at around the same time and run into him every morning. I was not dressed properly because I went to swim before going to work. I did not have my socks, tie, or belt on.

Henry wore a homburg in winter and a boater in summer, and always looked as fresh as if he had been awake at least for two hours. For months I could not figure out who Henry really was. There are many mysterious characters in New York.

Most of the major companies in Japan have their headquarters in Tokyo, but it is different in America. There are few large companies in New York other than financial firms. Those who had remained stubbornly in New York until about three years ago moved out then. Housing and commuting are both difficult in New York, just like Tokyo. It is not unusual to spend one hour commuting. One difference from Tokyo is that most people can sit down on a long-distance commuting train. But those who work on Wall Street also have to change from train to subway, and the subway gets quite crowded. Another contributory factor to the exodus of companies from New York is the sky-high rent for office space. Activities still remaining in New York are: security firms on Wall Street, banks on Park Avenue, public relations firms on Madison Avenue, department stores and other shops on Fifth Avenue, artists in Greenwich Village, actors and actresses on Broadway, the pornographic industry in Times Square, and the lawyers, doctors, and dentists who exist in superfluity all over New York.

What's interesting about New York is that working for a major company does not mean anything there. An unbelievable variety of occupations and races are gathered in New York. After spending three days there, some people become disgusted with the city and others fall in love with it. New York may be a difficult city to adapt to for those who are bothered by a slightly crooked frame on the wall, or who, when they forget to put an "s" at the end of a verb in the third person singular, start all over again—like blood type A people. And it may be a comfortable place to live in for those who do not mind wearing two different kinds of cuff-links when one of a set is missing, or who do not mind a jacket and trousers of different shades of blue—like blood type O people. But then, my doctor friend says that there is no scientific grounds for personality divination by blood types.

Although Henry looks mysterious, he turns out to be a successful businessman who owns a magazine company. When he came to Washington not too long ago, he gave me a copy of a newly published book of short stories edited by him.

In America, politicians, scholars, and businessmen tell a witty story at the start of a speech. A Japanese-style speech that begins with a conventional phrase such as "Pardon me from speaking from higher up than my superiors," and ends, after delivering a lengthy speech, with "Though short, this is my message," is not appreciated in America. You must begin with a witty short story or say something humorous to make the audience laugh, depending on the occasion. For instance, if the speaker is so short that the audience can only see his head above the rostrum, he could say "Ladies and gentlemen, I am standing," and the audience would burst into laughter. It will ease the tension in the audience, because not only the speaker is tense but also the audience. If a speaker can make the audience laugh with his first few words, then the speech is a success. The book edited by Henry, *This One Word Makes People Laugh* is a necessity for those who often deliver speeches.

I am sometimes asked to give speeches. I recently heard a story I thought I could use in my speech: A doctor said to his patient, "I have some good news and some bad news to tell you. Which would you like me to tell you first?" "Good news first, please," said the patient. "You have five more days to live . . ."

The patient, astounded, asked impatiently, "What is the bad news then?" The doctor replied gently, "I received this report four days ago." If you use this story at the start of a speech on U.S.-Japan economic friction and continue "Have U.S.-Japan relations soured to such an extent that they can disintegrate in one day just like the life of this patient?" the audience will listen intently. However, it may not always be successful. I gave a speech in New Orleans the other day in front of about 100 people. I wanted to explain U.S.-Japan relations clearly and began with that story. I was expecting the audience to roar with laughter, but they all looked terribly serious. It seemed that I was the only one who enjoyed the joke, so I felt embarrassed. A chill was cast over the audience and the mood did not change throughout my speech. Afterwards, I tried to think calmly why they did not laugh at my joke. Six thousand urologists were gathered there from all over the world. Dr. George Nagamatsu, who asked me to give the speech, is a world-famous urologist. My story was not something laughable for doctors who unfortunately sometimes have to give a patient a death sentence. I had forgotten the rule of "adapt your speech to the audience."

Eulogy on a "Smokestack"

Right in front of me was Central Park. The leaves had fallen and the horse-drawn carriages were passing over them. Drivers wearing tophats sat in the coaches, with their faces expressionless, waiting for passengers. The horses were all fat and big without exception. The air was chilly, but the sky was blue and clear, and the sun was shining over everything. It was before seven o'clock in the morning, but there were already quite a few joggers and people walking dogs in Central Park.

I pushed the revolving door of the New York Athletic Club with all my strength to let myself in. I showed my membership card to the intimidating receptionist, and he signaled me OK with his eyes. A jacket and tie must be worn in order to enter into the club.

There was no one in the high-ceiling lobby. Perhaps Dr. George Nagamatsu had gone directly to the swimming pool. My spirits were high with the anticipation of swimming for the first time in so long. After taking a shower, I started doing some warming-up exercises in the nude when Dr. Nagamatsu walked in. He had his front covered with a towel. It is a men's club and everybody is in the nude, just like at the public bath in Japan. The difference is that Americans do not cover their front. They walk around with their genitals exposed and dangling. Since Dr. Nagamatsu is a urologist, he must handle quite a few of them every day. But that does not mean that he does not feel embarrassed at the sight. He is a Japanese-American born in Seattle, but perhaps it is his upbringing that makes him bashful. He was brought up by his parents who came from Fukuoka, Kyushu.

I sank gradually into the water which was clear and pleasantly cold. I started off to the middle of the swimming pool. It is an ecstatic moment. I have swum in a great number of indoor swimming pools, but this one is the best. I felt happy. I swam in the nude and it made me reminisce of my childhood days when I used to swim in the river.

I swam to my heart's content. Then I took a shower with Dr. Nagamatsu. I washed his back thoroughly with a coarse nylon towel, and he washed my back in return. His skin was extremely elastic for his age.

I sat at the breakfast table feeling exhilarated. Dr. Nagamatsu drank his tomato juice and went off for another appointment. I was left with two ladies from Japan. "Did it feel nice?" asked a 49-year-old newscaster. "Tell me, do you really mean that you were stark-naked?" pursued a 35-year-old secretary. "I wonder if anyone swims backstroke there." "If so, I wonder if it looks like the smokestack on a ship. Oh . . . how disgusting!" I said nothing. The two women giggled. I almost said, "Of course some people swim backstroke. But they don't have erections when swimming." But I decided not to say anything. It was hard to believe that women of their age would be so innocent as to really believe this idea of the smokestack. I figured that they were only saying that knowing that it was not true. They would laugh scornfully if I said anything like that. When with women, if you are not certain whether you should speak or not, it is safer to say nothing.

In regard to whether or not they have an erection like a smokestack, there are all sorts of situations which only men would understand. There are many stories concerning the matter. Some of them are so painful that you cannot laugh. I was watching television in my hotel room in New York last night. "Now we have a story on people who are suffering from an illness which they cannot tell anyone else about," an attractive newscaster said. After a moment's hesitation, she added, lowering her voice, "Impotence." Immediately afterwards, commercials followed.

I have heard so much about impotence from Dr. Nagamatsu. Also with prostatitis, impotence is an illness often discussed in conferences on urology. "I wonder if it is possible to find the spot which, when touched, makes a man excited, or the nerve in the brain that will stimulate a man merely by hearing a woman's voice on the telephone," the Doctor said. I could tell by his eyes, behind his glasses, that he was not altogether joking.

In America, impotence can be a reason for divorce. Any man will fully understand the frustration an impotent married man must feel. A plastic bar can be implanted in the penis. But it will be exactly like a smokestack, standing erect all the time, and will be extremely inconvenient in one's daily life. So, a hinge is included to allow erection only when necessary. Dr. Nagamatsu says that it is not an uncommon operation.

Since men are full of curiosity where sex is concerned, every man has a certain knowledge of female anatomy. Women, on the other hand, think it is obscene even to study sexuality. Consequently, they know nothing about it. Sex education is important, perhaps not only for children, but also for adult women. I am for women's liberation and equal rights, but often I wish that women would learn about men even half as much as men learn about women. The proprietress of a bar in Tokyo once said to me, "Those two balls, I always thought that they are hanging vertically, like dumplings on a skewer. If they are placed horizontally, side by side, they will be in the way when you walk, won't they?" This is how much women know about men. Or I wonder if she was only kidding me.

Tranquilizers

On Friday, December 13, 1974, I was driving, as usual, from Wall Street to West Side Highway, from where I could see George Washington Bridge toward the mouth of the Hudson River on the left. The suspension bridge, which was illuminated by numerous lights, stood sharply outlined against the night sky.

My heart had been beating violently, and I was having difficulty breathing as I drove. I swallowed two tranquilizer pills my doctor had prescribed for times like this. I was 43 years old, and I was leading such a hectic life as the President of Nomura Securities International, Nomura's U.S. subsidiary and flag ship in the U.S. market, that it would not have been totally surprising if I had suddenly died of fatigue.

I parked my car in the basement garage and went to my apartment. "I am exhausted. Besides, it is Friday the 13th. I am going to bed now. Don't wake me up even if someone calls from Japan," I said to my wife and retired to the bedroom.

The next morning my wife said with a serious face, "Last night, after you went to bed, Chizuko called and said that your mother had suffered a minor stroke. She is in a hospital and she is going to be all right. But Chizuko wanted to let you know the telephone number of the hospital and the name of the doctor." My 74-year-old mother lived alone in a single house in Sano, in Tochigi Prefecture. But she was not totally alone because she ran a small knitting school, and was surrounded by some ten young women during the day and in the evening.

Ever since I was a little child I had a very close relationship with my mother, having been brought up by her as an only child, and she was always on my mind. Despite the high cost of the telephone bills, I habitually called my mother at least once a week and talked for half an hour. My cousin Chizuko who knew how close I was to my mother, must have called for fear that I would be worried to get no answer when I called her as usual.

My wife and children began to worry because I had been looking blankly out of the window since morning. "Why don't you go to Sano if you are so worried. Your mother will be delighted to see you," my wife said.

On Sunday, December 15, I departed from JFK Airport on a Pan American flight, and arrived at Haneda at five o'clock the next afternoon. Mr. Sueno from Nomura Securities met me at the airport and drove me directly to Sano. I arrived at Sano Kosei Hospital at around nine o'clock to find my mother with a thin coat of rouge and thick coat of lipstick. "How are you?" I asked, and she, without saying a word, lifted her right hand slightly. I could see her pink nightdress. I held her hand, feeling a little embarrassed because there was a nursing orderly beside the bed. "I am all right now," my mother uttered a word for the first time. Her speech was a little slurred. I knew she was dressed up for me because I had called her doctor from New York, and had informed him of my plan to visit her.

I did not see any point in going to my mother's house without her, so I decided to stay in a business hotel in the city. I had quite a lot of the brandy I had bought in New York and went to bed.

At six o'clock in the morning of Tuesday, the 17th of December, although I feared it might be too early, I went to the hospital. My mother was washing her face with the help of the orderly. "Did you sleep well?" she asked me, and I said "Yes, I slept soundly." Breakfast was brought in at seven o'clock. Rice, miso soup with seaweed, dried horse mackerel, pickles, and an apple. "They serve breakfast early in hospitals, don't they? It doesn't look bad," I said, and my mother said "You can have it, Yoshio. I don't want any." Her speech did not sound as badly slurred as last night. Or perhaps my ear was getting used to it. I sat in a chair by her bed and talked till noon. We did not speak about anything of substance, but only talked in a rambling way with frequent pauses.

"Mother, how would you rate me as a son, on a scale from one to one hundred?"

"Well, maybe about 70."

I was not exactly expecting a perfect score but I thought she was being pretty severe to give me only 70.

Her lunch was served and I ate it. A while later, the doctor came in to check. He asked my mother how she was feeling and took her pulse and was gone. I followed him and asked, "How is she?" "She should be all right unless something exceptional happens. You can go back to New York," the doctor said, smiling.

At around five in the afternoon, Chizuko's husband Hitoshi came to visit. My mother said to Hitoshi, "Take Yoshio out to dinner. He had hospital food for breakfast and lunch." "Sure, sure. Shall we go then, Yoshio-kun?" Hitoshi said in his naturally loud voice. I followed after him. As I left the room, I glanced back at my mother. She had a very complex expression and I could not tell if she was smiling or sobbing.

Hitoshi, Chizuko, and I went to a Japanese restaurant in the city and had pork cutlets and beer. The beer somehow did not make me feel good. At around nine, Hitoshi took me back to the hospital. I changed to slippers at the entrance and went to the third floor in the elevator. As I left the elevator, I saw in the dark a figure in a white apron walking toward me in the long corridor. "Your mother has just passed away," she said in a shaky voice. I put my hand in my trouser pocket to feel for the tranquilizers I had brought from New York.

The Aiseido Gynecologist

I feel intimidated by doctors. When I was a junior high-school student I seriously thought about becoming a doctor. There were some indications that my mother wanted me to be one, too. She was willing to buy me things like an anatomy kit for biology class. My mother was a nurse in a hospital in Hiroo, Tokyo, when she was young, and I suppose she had had an admiration for doctors since then.

As a junior high-school student, because we did not have a telephone in the house, I used to cycle to the Aiseido Gynecologist's office very often for my mother, who was in delicate health. The "Senior Doctor of Aiseido," which is what my mother called him, was tall and moustached. He made house calls on a bicycle. A specially made wire basket was attached to the bicycle under the handle-bars and he would carry his bulky black leather bag in it. I would offer the doctor a washbowl filled with hot water and soap when he finished examining my mother. He took time to wash his hands thoroughly. He never touched the tea and cake we had offered but left immediately, saying, "Take care."

When I accompanied my mother to see the doctor, we used to enter from the main entrance, where there was a wooden sign that read "Aiseido Gynecologist" written in large characters. It was a wooden, Western-style building, painted white. There was a Japanese-style lattice door in the alley next to the building, and that was where I used to enter when I went to see the doctor's oldest son "Akiba-kun." Since the doctor was called "Senior

Doctor" there must have been a "Junior Doctor," but I never saw one. "Akiba-kun" was my classmate in junior high school.

Doctors' sons usually become doctors. When we were in the 11th grade "Akiba-kun" applied to enter a private medical school in Tokyo. He strongly suggested that I also apply to the school, and kindly had an application form sent to me. I gave it some serious thought but decided against it in the end because I was not sure if I could afford it and, more than anything else, because I was not confident that I could follow this profession for a lifetime. One is confined in a room with patients day in and day out, examining them and making diagnoses. If a diagnosis is mistaken, a patient may die. Of course there may also be the chance to save lives, which would make one proud to be a doctor. But when I weighed these in the balance, my fear of misdiagnosing was heavier than the pleasure of saving lives.

The day I had been dreading came at last when I had to give a talk in front of 200 Japanese doctors at St. Moritz Hotel in New York. Some of the doctors had studied in Japan and others in America, and some were second- or third-generation Japanese-Americans. They all resided in the city or suburbs of New York. There were 30 round tables, at each of which ten people were seated. The hall was filled with doctors and their spouses. To my right was Dr. George Nagamatsu, a urologist, and to my left was my wife. "You are nervous, aren't you? You feel intimidated by doctors," my wife said, and she was right.

An American businessman of my age was complaining the other day, "I am really annoyed by my wife because lately she often says things as if she can read my mind. What is even more annoying is that what she says is almost always right." After 20 or 30 years of marriage, you begin to know your spouse inside-out. No, four or five years is enough for the wives to know their husbands, but in 20 or 30 years they become brazen in saying things which their husbands do not want to hear, while the husbands begin to feel a rapid decline in energy and strength. They do not have energy left to argue, even when touched on a sore spot by their wives, and they do nothing but nod. This is a phenomenon seen both in America and in Japan.

The turkey dinner was delicious. When the dessert was served, Dr. Nagamatsu stood up, walked to the rostrum and introduced me to the crowd. His posture and firm step made him look much younger than his 85 years. It was my turn. Bracing myself, I stood up. "President Carter tells a joke at the start of his speech that he thinks is very witty, but no one laughs. But there was one occasion when the audience roared with laughter, and that was when he spoke to the Japanese people in Tokyo. President Carter, naturally very pleased, asked the interpreter, a young Japanese woman, how she interpreted what he had said, and she replied 'I didn't understand a word of what you said, so I begged the audience to break into a roar of laughter.' " I told the story Mr. Carter had told me himself at the end of last year. Needless to say, my intention was to make the audience laugh. Since there were quite a few Americans among the doctors' spouses, I delivered my speech in English. They burst into laughter and I felt relieved. Then I spoke about what I thought of Japan-U.S. relations after the Gulf War.

My ophthalmologist, who performed an operation on my cataract; my dentist, whom I see two or three times a month; my internist, who conducts an endoscopy on me once a year; my urologist, who examines my prostate—all these doctors who have a thorough knowledge of my body were gazing at me. I was not sure if they enjoyed my speech. I feel intimidated by doctors.

Part Two

Life in Washington

4

Working in D.C.

Morning at the Watergate

I leave my apartment rubbing my sleepy eyes at six-thirty in the morning and find my way to the Watergate Hotel. Every morning I swim at the health club in the basement of the hotel. Henry, the receptionist, who looks very much like Giant Baba,* greets me, saying, "It's a nice day, isn't it?" I am still half asleep and barely manage to mumble "Yes." I used to swim naked at my athletic club in New York since all the members there were male. But at the Watergate I have to wear my swimming trunks because it is a coed facility. Only three or four people come at such an early hour. As the swimming pool has six lanes, there is no need to wait. The length of the pool is 18 meters and I do sixty lengths (30 laps). I usually swim breaststroke, but occasionally I do free style.

Among the members here are quite a few Senators, Congressmen, and lawyers. Mr. Saito, a Japanese lawyer, is also a member. When I occasionally see him, he always seems to be talking happily to Americans who appear to be members of the Congress. I have never really spoken to any of the members whom I see almost every morning. I assume they swim everyday because they lead sedentary lives, attending meetings from morning until night, and find the swimming a pleasant exercise. They must be addicted, like I am, I suppose.

*Giant Baba: famous Japanese professional wrestler

I was drying myself after a shower when I heard three Americans arguing excitedly. They were talking about Mayor Marion Barry's problems. For a time, Washingtonians seemed to be talking more about this notorious mayor than about President Bush. Incredibly, it was disclosed that the mayor, who had been campaigning against drug abuse among Washington's youth, was a drug user himself.

I asked a taxi driver one day what would become of Mayor Barry. He explained to me that Barry was more guilty on account of his lying to children than on account of his drug abuse. He sounded highly intelligent and I asked him what his background was. He was a policeman until only a year ago, he replied.

It is only eight o'clock in the morning but the air is already muggy. The summer has already started in Washington. A man at the entrance of the building looked familiar. It was Alan Greenspan, Chairman of Federal Reserve Board. Among other residents of this building are Barber Conable, President of the World Bank; Enrique Iglesias, President of Inter-American Development Bank; and Senator Bob Dole. When Paul Volcker was the Chairman of Federal Reserve Board, his name was mentioned in the media as often as the President. It has been much quieter since Alan Greenspan took over the position, and this is better for the American economy, because it means the dollar is more stable now.

I walk to work at MIGA (Multilateral Investment Guarantee Agency). It is 1,600 steps, and it takes me 14 minutes. I make it a rule not to make any appointments before 10:00 AM. From 8:30 to 10:00 AM I scan through the *New York Times,* the *Wall Street Journal,* the *Washington Post,* and the *Financial Times,* and then go through my schedule with my secretary, Celia. Celia is from Trinidad-Tobago in the Caribbean. She is a tall, pretty woman with large eyes. She was educated in England and speaks the Queen's English. Every time she uses an English word that I don't know the meaning of, I hand my dictionary to her and she points out the word to me. I always think "It's a useful word to remember," but then it doesn't sink in. It is my ultimate goal to increase my English vocabulary, but it is not easy.

The telephone on my desk rings. Automatically, I reach out to pick it up. I don't seem to be able to get rid of my old habit from my Nomura days of answering the telephone as soon as it rings. Celia stops me saying, "No! Mr. Terasawa." She answers the telephone and asks the caller's name, affiliation, and the nature of the call, and writes them down. What if it is someone from Japan who does not speak English? It makes me nervous to think that they may hang up, feeling helpless if confronted by Celia's businesslike tone.

MIGA is an agency within the World Bank, a large international organization with a staff of about 7,000. There are three things I noticed when I started working here. First of all, there is an atmosphere everywhere of university studies, research, and legal activity. Each member of the staff is already successful as a lawyer, economist, or engineer. Secondly, the staff is very international, gathered from 153 member countries. You sometimes see people wearing turbans or saris. No one would pay attention even if a Japanese showed up at work in a kimono. There are so many cases of international marriages—Lebanese husband and Australian wife, Spanish husband and British wife, Italian husband and Japanese wife, and so on and so on. When you find yourself in such an environment, the concept of internationalization, now so popular in Japan, begins to sound like an old-fashioned word of about 50 years ago. And thirdly, there is devotion. The World Bank staff has to work in life-threatening situations. They travel to the third world many times a year having been inoculated against yellow fever, cholera, tetanus, polio, etc. This is called a "mission" in the World Bank, whereas in private firms they are called business trips. The word "mission" is used with a meaning akin to a group going to foreign countries to spread their belief. The journeys the World Bank staff makes are missions without personal profit for the economic development of the third world. I am surrounded by people of a kind you would never see on Wall Street. My life here is one of constant tensions and surprises.

Always Keep Your Wit

I find it difficult to know the right time to say to Americans "Call me Terry." It is not easy to judge if I should say it at the first meeting or after several meetings. It is an American custom to call each other by their first names. Most of the people I dealt with on Wall Street were Americans, so I called them by their first names. Since MIGA staff come from all over the world, they do not always call one another by their first names. Two years ago, in July 1988, I arrived in Washington. I met with Barber Conable, President of the World Bank. I could not possibly call him Barber at the first meeting. And yet, because I would be working closely with him, it would not be appropriate for me to keep on calling him Mr. Conable. I think it was at about our tenth meeting when Mr. Conable said "Call me Barber."

On Sunday, July 8, 1990, the day before the start of a summit meeting, there was a big photograph of Prime Minister Toshiki Kaifu on the front pages of both the *New York Times* and the *Washington Post.* It was a million-dollar Kaifu smile. He and President Bush called each other George and Toshiki. Ronald Reagan and Yasuhiro Nakasone started the custom of the American President and the Japanese Prime Minister calling each other by their first names. It shifted from Ron-Yasu to George-Noboru, then to George-Toshiki. I do not know what they called each other when Sosuke Uno was the Prime Minister.

Prime Minister Toshiki Kaifu was quite popular among people in Washington, especially among American journalists. "He is doing his best," "He seems to be the type who will carry out what he has promised." Such are the impressions they have about him. Furthermore, President Bush seemed to have a favorable feeling toward Prime Minister Kaifu.

You need to be in the right mood to call each other by first names. In America, people carry on conversation inserting the other person's first name every so often, just like the accompaniment to the shamisen. You do not just say "Good morning." It is not complete unless you say "Good morning, Toshiki." "Don't you think so, Toshiki?" "Am I wrong, Toshiki?" and so forth. You hear the name "Toshiki" mentioned 20 times during a 30-minute conference. It is not a question of right or wrong. It is simply an American custom.

If you did the same in Japan, however, you would sound terribly snobbish. When I was a student I joined the ESS (English Speaking Society) because I was very much interested in English. I peeped into their meeting-room to find students in black uniform calling each other "George" and "Tom." I could not bear the snobbery and immediately decided to quit the society.

On August 30, 1956, I departed for America from Yokohama on the *Hikawa-maru,* with a send-off to the tune of "Auld Lang Syne." My dream to study in the U.S. finally came true when I passed the Fulbright examination. During my 14-day voyage I discovered two things: one was how to use a Western style toilet—I had never used one until then. I had no choice because it was the only kind of toilet the ship had. The other thing was calling one another by first names. An American university professor on board advised me that in order to succeed in the U.S., you have to call one another by first names. "Your last name is Terasawa, so let's call you Terry." Thus, he kindly named me.

Celia suggested yesterday that we hold a going-away party for Paul, her assistant in MIGA. Coffee, tea, and cakes were put on the table. About ten secretaries gathered in the office. Americans love parties. They always find excuses for having parties. They have only the kinds of food and drinks that can be easily and inexpensively obtained. The best and most important part of parties is conversation, so food and drinks do not matter.

Paul worked for one year next to my office. When I was asked to give a toast, I realized that I did not know his last name. It is not unusual to know only first names. Someone may say "I have known Henry for over ten years, but come to think of it, I do not know his last name." I am not exaggerating. That would be something unheard of in Japan.

"I wonder why Americans call one another by their first names," I said to my American friends, and they said that it is probably because Americans come from all over the world, and some people have difficult-to-pronounce last names of German, French, or Dutch origin.

There is a weekly magazine called "The New Republic," which is widely read among politicians in Washington. Fred Barnes, who covers the White House, once wrote an article for the magazine in which he praised Prime Minister Kaifu. In the Bush-Kaifu meeting held in March in Palm Springs, Prime Minister Kaifu confessed in frank manner, "It was hectic with general elections in Japan until only a few days ago. I had to hustle about the country, dripping with sweat." President Bush smiled. A while later, President Bush rang Prime Minister Kaifu at the Hotel Okura, where he stayed on weekends, to seek conclusions on a political level on the Structural Impediment Initiative. "I feel relieved to hear that. I think I will be able to sleep soundly tonight," Prime Minister Kaifu said. President Bush apparently liked this kind of conversation with human touches. Barnes wrote in his article that it was because President Bush liked Prime Minister Kaifu that Japan was exempted from Super 301.*

*Super 301: U.S. law against trade practices deemed unfair to the U.S.

It is important not only in the U.S. but also in the international community to relax and have conversations interspersed with wit.

Blowing Your Own Trumpet

Restaurant Florian is a good place for entertaining guests. Both the food and service are good and it has a pleasant ambience. I was to have lunch with Mr. Battat, who earned his Ph.D. in Chinese economy from MIT and was a professor at a university in Indiana until a year ago. It is about a five-minute walk to the restaurant from MIGA. It was hot, but not intolerably so. In fact, it was not bad for August in Washington.

As we walked, I asked Mr. Battat, "Where were you born? What is your nationality?" He murmured, "I don't have a simple answer to your question. It is very complicated."

The restaurant was well air-conditioned. Madame Carlucci greeted us with a pleasant smile as usual. She is always dressed nicely. She is also an artist, and about 20 pieces of her work hang on the walls of the restaurant, mostly of flowers or women. "You are more beautiful than ever," I said to her. "Thank you very much," she said, winking. I wonder if it is because I have lived in America for so long, or because I am getting bold with age, that I can compliment women in this manner.

A tall, thin man strode up to us. It was the maitre d'hôtel. *"Ikaga desu ka?"* he greeted me in some Japanese he had just learned.

After we were seated, Mr. Battat answered my question. "I was born in Lebanon, and was educated in France. When I was 18, I came over to the States to continue my education."

"How many languages do you speak?"

"Seven—Arabic, Hebrew, French, Spanish, Italian, Chinese and English."

"In what language do you dream?"

"I have never thought about that. Perhaps sometimes in English and other times in Arabic."

There are many cosmopolitan people like Mr. Battat in the World Bank and MIGA. Many of them, especially those from small countries in Europe and the Middle East, speak numerous languages.

When I was a junior high-school student, I studied Esperanto, thinking that it was going to be an international language. Whatever happened to Esperanto? Without a doubt, English has become the international language. I often say to Americans, "I envy you. English is spoken everywhere in the world. You can use your own language in the most complex international conferences. You have a great advantage." Most of the Americans I know are intelligent people. They always say, "I feel deeply ashamed. Because we can use our own language anywhere in the world, we don't make the effort to learn foreign languages. We tend to think that the world is revolving around us. We have to be careful."

On the personal evaluation form of the World Bank and MIGA, there is a space for self evaluation. You evaluate yourself. I do not know about the younger generation, but Japanese people of my generation are not used to evaluating themselves or listing their own achievements. We feel that it is something others do for you. But self-evaluation is commonly done not only in the international organizations but also in the private firms and the banks in the U.S. Americans are trained from primary school to advertise themselves most effectively. I receive many CVs from college graduates, often with long lists of qualifications.

In Japan, a CV form of my generation had a space for awards and punishments. If you had had awards you had to list them. Likewise, if you had had punishments, you had to list them, too. In a self-evaluation form of my generation, there was a space for both qualities and faults. In America, they only mention awards and good points, which I think is unbalanced.

When I was still single, a plump middle-aged busybody came and showed me photos and the CV of a young lady whose background the woman said was impeccable. She was a graduate of one of the most prestigious universities and was good at all sorts of sports, was fluent in English, and had the modesty of a respectable Japanese lady, together with certificates for flower arrangement and the tea ceremony. Americans' CVs are just like the CVs Japanese prepare for arranged marriages. They only mention good things. Mr. Battat had told me: "I don't like self-evaluation. I was not trained to be a trumpeter."

In the Structural Impediment Initiative meetings, the Japanese Government blew its own trumpet: "Everything our government is doing is right." The U.S. Government blew its own trumpet even harder: "The U.S. Government is always right."

Society has changed. Nowadays you have to be self-aggrandizing, "I am such a wonderful woman," or "I have these capabilities," because no one else will do it for you. The same goes for countries. You will lose if you do not blow your own trumpet.

I grew up in a society where silence was golden and modesty was a virtue. Although I have been living in the States for many years, I will never become like an American.

Dinner Party Melancholy

A charcoal gray suit. A white shirt. Now what color tie goes well? Perhaps white polka dots on navy would be a safe choice. I do not have much time, so I need to use it efficiently. I take a shower first. I do not have time to look at my deteriorating body in the mirror or to weigh myself on a scale. Besides, I do not want to do that because I am afraid of what I will see. I used to wear Christian Dior cologne, but I do not any more. I never had much body odor, but as I withered with age, I now have none at all. Besides, I do not like perfume or cologne on either men or women. Perhaps it will be different when I am really old.

I brush my teeth. You have to be careful about bad breath when you speak with Americans, because they put their faces very close to yours. I had my teeth cleaned just yesterday. I should gargle with Listerine again before I leave.

I like black socks. My drawers are full of them. But there are thin ones and thick ones. It is difficult to sort them out after they come back from the laundry, and they become paired with the wrong ones. I realize that I have put a thin one on my left foot and a thick one on my right. I do not have time to change.

It is my dream to throw away all the socks I have and buy two dozen pairs of long black socks. Then I can be sure to wear the right pair. I usually wear the same suit for the evening as the one I wore earlier that day because it will still look clean. You can save money on the dry cleaning that way. But it just does not feel right tonight. I had sukiyaki for lunch in a Japanese restaurant. Perhaps my suit smells. I should not be a miser, but wear a clean suit that just came back from the dry cleaner. Men do not dress up for others, they dress up for themselves, I tell myself.

I have been invited to a dinner at an American home. It starts at seven, and there are ten couples. Until nine there are cocktails. People just talk and talk for two hours. I go to dinner parties by myself because my wife does not live in Washington. So I have to do all the talking.

It is impossible to understand English one hundred percent. Jokes, especially, are difficult to understand. I have to continue listening without interrupting even if I do not understand. If I interrupt every time I have a difficulty in understanding, conversation will not be carried on smoothly. People tell jokes to make others laugh. Everyone laughs because they find them funny, except me. But I do not think I should look serious when everyone else is laughing. So I try to laugh, and it makes me feel uncomfortable.

One gets tired of standing for two hours. There are chairs there but I cannot sit down, because people older than myself are still standing.

Finally, the dinner starts. I sit down feeling relieved. Wine is served. I politely decline, because I do not drink at all. There are an increasing number of people who do not drink, so I am excused without any problem.

People do not usually make speeches at dinner parties. In principle, you talk to those sitting next to you. You can talk on various topics, but you have to avoid the following: political opinions, criticizing certain countries or races, sex, illness, and gossip. Anything other than these is all right. But long stories are not appreciated. You talk for a minute or two and wait to see the reactions of the others. Monologue is not accepted. Dialogue is good.

A typical conversation might go like this: Mr. A: "My German friend was arrested for speeding while cycling in Frankfurt." Mr. B: "Really? He was cycling? Not driving?" Mrs. C: "Besides, there is no speed limit in Germany. I don't understand why they should have a speed limit for bicycles." People start showing interest. When you are asked to continue the story, you do so. Often people ask me to talk about Japanese history or culture, and then I always get depressed to realize how little I know about my own country.

It is already eleven o'clock when the dinner is over. I want to go home and stretch on my bed. But this is not easily achieved. There are still after-dinner drinks. Until about twenty years ago, men and women enjoyed coffee and brandy in separate rooms, and talked about different things. In those days, women talked about fashion, shopping, and cooking. Men talked about politics, economics, and books they had just read. It was easier for both men and women to stick to their own sex. But things are different now. Many women are professionals, and they may have greater knowledge than their husbands about political and economic issues. Consequently, men and women now have after-dinner drinks together.

This does not matter for me any more because I am old and I will soon be disappearing from this society, but I would like to advise young Japanese to develop the capacity to talk with foreigners on things of substance.

English and Golf Are Not Easy

On one side of the table were several people from Merrill Lynch, and on the other, several from Nomura Securities. I do not remember the details, but it was some kind of negotiation. The Nomura people were talking to one another in low voices. "Not a good idea to say that now." "Let's put it this way for now." They assumed that the American side would not understand what they were saying. When the morning session was over, one of the Merrill Lynch men gestured to me. He was young. I nodded and went into another room with him. He said, "I don't quite know how to say this, but I studied Japanese for three years at Yale and another three years at the University of Tokyo. I understand Japanese even when they murmur. I thought I would keep it secret but decided that it would not be fair." I broke into a cold sweat.

Luis Dodero, a legal consultant at MIGA, is Spanish. He told me: "We had negotiations in Spain with the Iraqis on a very complicated issue. One of us was fluent in Arabic. When the negotiations were over, Iraqis distributed the transcript in Arabic and Spanish. We were all given the Spanish version except for this man who was fluent in Arabic. How they knew he could read Arabic is still a mystery to me. He never uttered a word in Arabic. I was puzzled."

It is very hard to master foreign languages. I wonder how high a level one can reach in them. Sometimes I feel depressed by my inability in English. I was very much interested in the language. I studied it very hard ever since junior high school. I participated in English speech contests. I took extra courses in English in language schools. I studied for a Fulbright fellowship, which I passed, and was given an opportunity to study at the University of Pennsylvania for one year. I have been living in the U.S. for almost 20 years. Nevertheless, I still have difficulties in English.

My wife would ask me, watching a movie on television, "What did he say?" I would say "Shush. Later. Don't disturb me now." To tell you the truth, I did not understand it myself. But it would hurt my dignity as a man to admit it. She may ask me later when the movie is over. I tell myself that I will deal with it then.

I do not have any problems when intelligent people speak in standard English on general subjects. However, I am lost when people speak very fast, with an accent, or on a subject with which I am not familiar. Familiar subjects for me are limited to the following: Wall Street business talks, the Third World and industrialized countries, and U.S.-Japan trade issues. Sometimes I find it refreshing to hear something with which I am totally unfamiliar, such as the young soldiers' dialogue in Vietnam war movies, American teenagers' language on television, or the humor of popular comedians.

There is something in common between my English and my golf. I have been dealing with both of them for more than 30 years, I am interested in both, and I do not seem to improve in either. I wonder why. In the case of my English, probably the problem is my limited vocabulary. I always carry a small dictionary with me, and whenever I come across a word that I do not know the meaning of, I look it up in the dictionary. Alas, I am OLD. I often check the same word over and over again. It is so discouraging. You must learn languages when you are young. Sometimes I wonder if I am incapable. My children have been studying English less than ten years but they can already laugh watching the television. Because it hurts my dignity, I do not ask them what is so funny. Sometimes they just go ahead and explain it to me.

The same goes for my golf. What I understand in theory is not always easy in practice. The young people to whom I was giving instruction last year have already surpassed me.

"I miss Japan," said a friend who had just spent a three-week holiday in Tokyo. "Japanese food is good, and more than anything else, I don't have a language problem there." I could not agree more. When I go back to Tokyo, I wake up at around five o'clock in the morning because of the time difference, and I turn on the television and watch it as if possessed. I find every program so very interesting.

Japan has become an economic superpower. Japanese politicians bring simultaneous interpreters with them when they visit Washington, and Japanese businessmen do the same when they visit New York. I can understand very well what is being said when I listen to the interpreters. If you speak in Japanese they immediately translate it into beautiful English. It makes me wonder if there is any point at all in making efforts to learn English. When I speak I always wonder if I should use English or Japanese. If I speak in Japanese, it will be translated into correct English. But I always choose English because I somehow believe that I will sound more convincing if speak in my own words, even if they are not very polished.

I will never be able to speak English as well as I speak Japanese. It will never happen. But I still cling to my little dictionary. The same will be true with my golf.

The Limit of Patience

The Japanese expression—*rashiku* (-like), such as in lady-like, child-like, is not easy to translate into English. In Japan, for example, there is a preconceived idea of the way a woman should be, and if a woman does not behave in accordance with this concept, then, she will be considered "unladylike." A woman has to behave gracefully and has to be good at every kind of household task. If a boy kicks a door open with his foot, people will say that he is a lively boy. But if a girl did the same, they would criticize her for being unfeminine.

It is different in the U.S. For instance, in primary school, girls sit cross-legged, just like boys, when they listen to their teachers. And the teachers do not scold the girls for doing so. In this competitive society, women will not be able to emulate men unless they are educated to be dauntless and courageous rather than graceful. Women's liberation is definitely reflected in education.

A boss, no longer able to stand the way a female staffer dressed for work, told her to go to a charm school to become more ladylike. The girl, infuriated, did not waste any time in suing the firm. She won the case and received $2 million. This is a true incident that took place recently in Washington, D.C.

In Japan, you can guess people's professions by the way they look, such as "doctor-like" or "pro-golfer-like." And they carry the "face" for their profession at all times. Doctors wear white coats, and maintain a dignified face as they see their patients. Pro-golfers can be distinguished easily by their extraordinarily sun-tanned faces and their mannerisms. In America, doctors do not necessarily wear white coats, and when they get to know their patients better, they may say something like "I too have a high cholesterol level and am taking medicine for that." The myth I had believed, that doctors are God-like people who never become ill, crumbles in my mind, and I feel relieved. Even pro-golfers, when you dine with them, talk about things other than golf, which makes me think that they might be successful if they switched their profession and became stockbrokers. In other words, they are normal people.

There are times when it works disadvantageously to appear to be something other than what you are. Many of the Japanese children born and raised in the U.S. cannot read or write Japanese. They can speak the language because their parents speak it at home, but they cannot read it. Such a child took a train in Japan and arrived at a station. But he could not read the sign. He asked a railman where he was. The railman gave him a contemptuous look and said bluntly, "It's written there," because the boy had a Japanese face. The boy who could not read it, feeling helpless, was close to tears.

Approximately 6,000 Japanese live in the Washington metropolitan area. Most of them live in houses in the suburbs. Because there are not as many and as varied restaurants as in New York, they entertain guests at home. And of course they invite guests in couples.

At these parties you sometimes hear a man say, "We owe the nation's economic success to the women who supported their husbands. We must thank the wives gathered here." The other men nod, agreeing somewhat that perhaps it is so, but still feeling a little dubious. They listen quietly to the man, wondering how he could say such a thing nonchalantly in front of his wife, and feeling slightly uncomfortable. What the man says is not wrong. When I was growing up, both men and women knew their places, and women's liberation did not exist. Knowing that women kept the house completely reliably, men could spend all their energy on their work. Things are quite different now in America, and American husbands are not as fortunate as Japanese.

Over 30 years ago, when I was studying in Philadelphia, some kind Americans used to invite foreign students to their homes. One Sunday, I was invited to a picnic by an American couple with two children. Bob, the husband, came in a big station wagon to pick me up at my dormitory early in the morning. Then he and I went to his house to pick up his wife and their six-year-old and their six-month-old baby, and drove to Fairmont Park in Philadelphia. I still remember vividly how hard he worked that day. He loaded the station wagon with a playpen, an iron hibachi (a hibachi to a Japanese is a large ceramic bowl in which you burn charcoal in ashes as a heater, but Americans, for some reason, call a small barbeque grill a hibachi) and many other things. He had to do it all by himself because his wife was busy with the two children. When we arrived at the park, he worked like a beaver, dripping with sweat, assembling the playpen and starting the fire in the hibachi. When we returned home from the picnic, Bob brought the things back in the house, and without taking a rest, went to the kitchen to make coffee. Then he kissed his wife and said "I love you." I just stood there in blank amazement, wondering if every American husband worked as hard as Bob, or if he was exceptional.

In contrast, Japanese husbands were fortunate, for they could concentrate on their work without having to worry about the household affairs. However, the ladylike women who made all that possible and who knew their places no longer exist. The society has changed. What is frightening is that the model Japanese wives who submissively bore their burdens have reached the limit of their patience and are vigilantly seeking an opportunity to abandon their husbands.

Man and the Tuxedo

The odor of mothballs struck my nose when I entered the elevator. Inside were several red-faced men dressed in tuxedos or double breasted jackets with white ties, and smiling women in kimonos with border patterns, holding packages wrapped in red-and-white *furoshiki.** Perhaps they had just come from a wed-

* *Furoshiki:* cloth used for wrapping and carrying packages

ding reception. This is a familiar sight in hotels in Tokyo. I do not know the average amount of wedding expenses, but I assume that it is enormous. Since I have three young unmarried daughters, this is a matter of direct concern to me.

More men seem to wear tuxedos than tailcoats now. When I married thirty years ago, no one wore a tuxedo. At that time, some men who had spent some time in America formed a "Tuxedo Club." Its purpose was the rather insignificant one of having dinner together once a month wearing tuxedos. I was invited to become a member, but I declined because I found it embarrassing. The members of the Club, clad in tuxedos, when strolling through a hotel lobby, conscious of other people's eyes and yet feeling excited, might be called by a woman who looked like a bar proprietor, "Hello, you, bellboy over there." But they did not mind.

There is something about the tuxedo that excites men. I can understand men who want to dress up in them. Rich women living in suburban Hollywood fly to San Francisco to see the opera just because they want to wear fur coats. Los Angeles' all-year-long warm weather does not give them opportunities to wear a fur coat. Perhaps men's desire to wear a tuxedo is not as strong as that of women to wear a fur coat, but nevertheless I wonder what causes it. Broad-chested men look good in a tuxedo, and the older men get, the better it suits them.

I bought my tuxedo in Brooks Brothers in New York when I was 40 years old. I bought it thinking it might be a waste because I would not wear it very often. "I wonder if I need a summer tuxedo and a winter tuxedo," I murmured as if talking to myself, and a salesman said, with a puzzled look, "There aren't such things as summer or winter tuxedos."

Summer in New York does not get as humid as in Tokyo, so you need not wear extremely thin suits. Although it gets very cold in winter in New York, since houses are heated, almost to the point that you sweat, you do not need very thick suits either.

There are, however, summer suits and winter suits. But there is not a set date for changing clothing for the season as in Japan, where everyone changes to summer clothing on June 1st and to winter clothing on October 1st. Throughout the year, summer and winter suits, both of which are made with materials that are hardly different from each other, hang in the closet. Even in winter, if it is unseasonably warm, one wears a summer suit, and in summer if you are going to a place which is intensively air conditioned, you wear a thicker suit. In San Francisco, where there can be four seasons in one day, people wear a summer suit during the day and a winter suit at night. Americans do not put their clothes away at the end of each season, with mothballs in the garment boxes. The smell of mothballs is very Japanese.

I wore my tuxedo most recently on the occasion of IMF-World Bank Annual Meeting. The Annual Meeting is held annually in September in Washington, D.C., for two consecutive years and then in a city outside the U.S. and again twice in Washington, D.C., and then in another city, and so on. Recent locations outside Washington have included Toronto in 1982, Seoul in 1985, Berlin in 1988, and Bangkok in 1991. Berlin still had the wall when the annual meeting was held there in 1988. Back then, no one predicted the early reunification of East and West Germany. The Annual Meeting is scheduled to be held in Madrid in 1994.

Finance ministers and presidents of central banks of the more than 150 member countries attend the IMF-World Bank Annual Meeting. It is equivalent to the general stockholders' meetings in private firms. The Managing Director of the IMF and the President of the World Bank report on operations to the "representatives of stockholders" from each country, and finance ministers deliver speeches on issues of world economy, finance, and development. Finance Minister Ryutaro Hashimoto attended the meetings in 1989 and 1990.

The dinner held on the day of the annual meeting is a "black tie optional" which means you can wear a tuxedo, but you do not have to. If the invitation says "black tie," you are expected to wear a tuxedo, and you will feel embarrassed if you wear only a business suit.

The shirt to wear with a tuxedo has vertical pleats in the front, and the first three buttons are black ornamental ones. It is not an easy job to button up these three ornamental buttons. Never in my life have I been able to button them up without any difficulty. I always get irritated and become unable to do it smoothly. And whenever I have to wear a tuxedo I seem to be in a hurry. Irritation turns to anger and then to distress, and at the end I feel like giving up totally.

I was determined not to repeat this agonizing process tonight and started getting dressed 30 minutes earlier. I was calm and so was able to do up the button in no time. It is vital to stay calm in doing anything.

The dinner party was very enjoyable. Five violinists and two cellists played my favorite pieces such as "Domino," "La Comparsita," and music from "Cats."

A Ten-year Diary

The year 1991 has begun at last. A friend sent me a ten-year diary. It is the size of a weekly magazine and each page is divided into ten sections. The page for January 1st has ten columns from 1991 to 2000. I turn 60 on October 3rd this year, so this diary will be the record of my 60s, if I can keep the diary every day for ten years. I murmur to myself, looking at the diary, that it will not last very long. Yet, if I wrote in it every day, even only two or three lines a day, it would make me feel good afterwards. No, no, I could not possibly keep it up for ten years. Besides, I may not live another ten years. In a couple of years, when I write about what happens on a particular day, because I can read about the same day a year or two years previously, I may pretend and try to make the new day sound better than those of the past. Or I may not feel like writing anything at all, feeling despondent comparing the day with previous years when things were going well. I should not write anything that I do not want anyone else to read. You cannot keep a diary if you lead a life with a guilty conscience.

One way to keep a diary is to write about your physical condition each day. It does not have to be long, you can write something like "slight diarrhea," "sore throat," or "palpitation and irregular pulse." This will give you a clear record of the deteriorating state of your health.

There is something called a "dream diary." You write down any dream you remember immediately after you wake up. It is easier said than done. But Musei Tokugawa* is said to have kept one. If one kept both "a diary of real life" and "a diary of dreams" for twenty or thirty years, they would make very useful materials for psychology.

Like Japanese businessmen, most American businessmen carry a pocket diary with them at all times in which they enter appointments and conference notes and so forth. Tentative appointments are penciled in. At that point, the appointment is not one hundred percent definite. When it is confirmed, it is written down with a pen.

Suppose you meet an old classmate at a party and talk about playing golf together and, checking your schedule of three or four months ahead, both you and your classmate "pencil in" the plan in your pocket diaries.

The decisive difference between secretaries to American businessmen and those to Japanese businessmen is that the former have the authority to pencil in while the latter do not. Japanese

---

*Musei Tokugawa: An entertainer and writer, 1894–1971

companies have an "organization" called the secretarial section. Suppose a Miss Yamamoto is one of the staff of the section and happens to work for a Mr. Tanaka. When she quits her job to marry, the head of the section assigns a Miss Suzuki to replace Miss Yamamoto in working for Mr. Tanaka.

For some ten years, Nancy had been secretary to Donald Regan, President of Merrill Lynch. When Regan was nominated to be Treasury Secretary by former President Ronald Reagan, Nancy left Merrill Lunch to work as secretary to Treasury Secretary Donald Regan.

In America, the relationship between bosses and secretaries is very personal. A secretary who has been working for many years for the same boss knows everyone from personal friends to business contacts, and can use her own judgment to pencil in. Because the boss trusts his secretary's ability and personality, he authorizes her to pencil in.

In Japan, almost always, the secretary to a chairman or company president is male. It is not because women are considered inferior, but because men find male secretaries more convenient and comfortable to be with when traveling or attending meetings. If the climate of suspicion surrounding a boss and his female assistant traveling together by Shinkansen or plane could be eliminated, it would be ideal for top executives to have female secretaries who are fluent in English and could act as interpreters when required to do so, or could work as a secretaries exercising their feminine intuition.

I went back to Tokyo for one week at the end of the year for the New Year's holiday. On the first of January my son and I paid a visit to Hikawa Shrine in Koenji, which is dedicated to my guardian god. I saw some local people enjoying a bonfire in the shrine precinct. They appeared to be burning talismans and charms from the previous year. After the visit, we drove on Ome Avenue toward Shinjuku. Traffic was extremely light even in Tokyo on New Year's Day. My son, who is a college freshman, was in the driver's seat of the red sports car and I had settled myself into the passenger seat. The sports car was very low on the ground and felt awfully fast. Somehow I became uneasy. Perhaps it was because I was not accustomed to riding in a sports car.

"You've got a Whitney Houston cassette, haven't you?"

"Yeah."

"Can I listen to it?"

I am an admirer of Whitney Houston since I heard her in a car five years ago on the way to Augusta, Georgia to watch the Masters' Golf Tournament.

I find it easier to talk to my son sitting side by side in a car than facing each other. We both feel a little embarrassed talking face to face. *Thirty Letters from a Businessman Father to His Son* must have become a bestseller, I think, because face-to-face dialogue between parents and children is difficult. Over forty years ago, Kimiko Hatano's *Boyhood,* which is letters exchanged between mother and son, became a bestseller.

Conversation between parents and children can be conducted better in a car sitting side by side, looking out of the window at the scenery, without any pose.

"When I was in primary school, it was a daily task to keep a diary. I didn't have anything special to write, so I wrote almost the same thing day after day like "I got up at such and such time, and went to school, then came home and went to bed at such and such time," my son told me, turning down the volume of the cassette. "There were kids in my class who kept interesting diaries and had them bound into books with a title *Record of My Six Years in Primary School* printed in gold letters at graduation." I wondered if it was difficult for my son, who was born and grew up in New York until the age of four, to keep a diary in Japanese, or if it was his way of expressing rebellion against such a dull task as keeping a diary.

5

Meeting People

An Old Lady with a Dog

I am an enthusiastic admirer of the actress Sadako Sawamura. Ms. Sawamura grew up in Shitamachi (the traditional shopping and entertainment districts of Tokyo—Asakusa, Ueno, Tsukiji, etc.) and later moved to Yamanote (the uptown, hilly residential sections of Tokyo).

One morning, she was sweeping the sidewalk in front of her Yamanote house when a man passed by. She said, "Good morning," just like she used to do in Shitamachi. The man looked surprised, and hurried away at a brisk pace. I wonder if anything strange like this happens in New York or Washington. Every morning on my way to the Watergate Hotel to swim I see a graceful, petite old lady with a Pekinese. I say "Good morning," to her, and the lady looks at me, smiling, and says "Good morning" to me. Occasionally I open a conversation with something like "What an adorable little dog!" and we talk for a few minutes.

In America, in residential areas, but perhaps not in business districts, strangers exchange greetings in a very natural way. My apartment is on the 11th floor. One morning I rushed into the elevator wearing a heavy overcoat, and a tall old lady inside it said, looking at my overcoat, "Good morning. It's going to be a warm day today. Day-time temperature is expected to be about 70°F (21°C)." Although I had never met this lady before, she is a tenant of the same apartment building and she talked about the weather in addition to a straightforward greeting. I ran back to my apartment and took off my overcoat.

On a golf course, whether you know one another or not, the moment you see someone, you say "Hello. How are you?" Even in Japan, in Tokyo Golf Club where I am a member, everyone greets one another with a "Good morning."

Mariko Miyagi* writes in her book *The Art of Socializing*, "Everyone on the elevator was staring at the door. No one said a word. I didn't like that. They were just looking at the floor numbers 1, 2, 3 . . . lighting up and no one uttered a sound. I really didn't like it. When they wanted to get off, they just pushed past the other people without saying anything. Why couldn't they say 'Excuse me.' It is particularly awkward when you happen to be on an elevator in a high-rise building of 30 or 40 floors, with only one other person. The two people look away from each other and neither of them says anything. And when one of them gets off, he or she just leaves without saying a word." This gives me the impression that Miss Miyagi is a very warm-hearted person.

Even in America, strangers do not speak to one another on the elevators in Wall Street. With blood-shot eyes they stare at the floor-number lights going on and off and say nothing at all. Especially during the recent days of recession, people's minds were closed off from each other. You have to have a calm and broad mind to be able to speak agreeably to strangers in such circumstances.

I am hopeless with anything technical—I cannot even change a fuse. I am a total failure in the information-oriented computerized society. I have tried to learn how to use personal computers several times, but I always ended by giving up in despair. Some people use a word processor very easily to prepare a manuscript, but I will never be able to do that. I am not boasting about the

---

*Mariko Miyagi: a popular actress

fact that I do not use a word processor, I honestly wish I could learn, but I have given up because I know I will never be able to do so.

In 1956 when I first came to America, there was a Nomura Securities man called Ono in New York. Nomura Securities was the first among Japanese companies to purchase large computers from UNIVAC. Ono was the head of the computer department and was sent to Wall Street to study how the security firms on Wall Street were utilizing computers. I was ordered to work as his interpreter but I felt completely lost because I had absolutely no knowledge of computers. I should have thought: it is the dawning of the age of computers, and high time for me to learn about them. But the truth was that I developed an aversion to computers and decided to stay away from them as much as possible. To me, the computer equates with a calculator. I feel daunted by the fact that things around us are becoming ever more computerized and ever more complex as a result. The VCRs and automobiles of about ten years ago are the easiest for me to operate. The mere sight of the most recent ones gives me a chill.

I do not think I am quite old enough to talk about the "good old days." So I do not really want to say it, but recently I feel that I am being left behind, and often think that things were better before. Five hundred years ago Columbus arrived in the American continent. But people around the world had no way of knowing immediately about the discovery because in those days there were no media like today's. The news was passed by word of mouth from person to person over the years.

In the morning, if one sees another human being where there is no other soul, he would hope to talk to the other, and if one's eye meets another's in an elevator, he would naturally smile. But today's world is no longer a place where that sort of normal human behavior is seen. Perhaps the computer has something to do with the transformation of society. No, I may be wrong. It is nothing but the prejudiced opinion of someone who is not at ease with machinery.

Anyway, I talk to strangers. I need to summon up my courage to do so, and sometimes I feel hurt at receiving a surly reaction. Despite all that I still talk to strangers. Someday something good will happen.

A Chest of Drawers and a Microwave Oven

The host greets you at the door when you are invited to an American home. Then his wife joins you and they take you around the house—bedrooms, bathrooms, living room, dining room, kitchen, study, recreation room, etc., all of which are kept very neat and tidy. In Japan, guests are shown to a Western-style reception room by the entrance or to a Japanese room with an alcove, and are served tea there. They would seldom, if ever, be taken around the other rooms of the home.

Each American home has its own individual personality, which differentiates it from all the others. And that is why Americans want to show off their homes to visitors, and the visitors in turn are curious to see how their hosts live. In Japan, although some people may be richer than others, and some live in larger homes, the structure of houses does not vary much, Besides, Japanese people are not very much interested in "dwelling." Therefore, they do not show off their homes and do not care to see the homes of others.

It is amazing how tidy the Americans keep their homes at all times. Of course they do tidy up when they invite guests, but the fact that their homes are so neat when they have guests means they keep them relatively tidy at all times. I think American men's hard work is attributable to the tidiness of their homes. Japanese men, fathers and sons, just drop their clothes when they undress and never put them in the closet, they never take dishes to the kitchen; they generally make a mess in the house. Women, mothers and daughters, clean up the mess made by men, and that is the tacit understanding between men and women in Japan. But in America, boys too are brought up to take care of themselves and to help with the household work.

I know a Japanese female doctor living in New York. "I make house calls to Americans' homes in emergency. I see my patients in their bedrooms, and I am always amazed to see how tidy the rooms are," she says.

Americans take good care of furniture. Apartments with windows facing south, which get plenty of sunshine, are relatively cheap because the sunlight could ruin the furniture. Furniture is seen as part of the body of the person who used it. A rocking chair a grandmother sat in day after day, looking at the flames in the fireplace, is the grandmother herself. And even after the grandmother is gone, the rocking chair remains where it was when she was alive. Her grandchildren can feel her warmth when they sit in the rocking chair. The oak desk grandfather used is where he did a lot of thinking, resting his chin in his hands, and it was also his grandfather's desk used during the Civil War.

In Japan, people buy furniture to match the house each time they move, whereas in America, people buy a house to match their furniture. Of course Americans do buy new furniture, but they do so with the intention of using it for their lifetime. And they take good care of it.

When American companies transfer their employees overseas, the expenses of shipping furniture are all taken care of by the company. In principal, when Americans move to Europe or Japan, they take their furniture with them. Their life would not be the same without their furniture.

After the war, the Japanese built everything anew, trying to adopt the modern, and discarding the old. People in the countryside replaced their old wooden chests of drawers with steel ones. Now, pieces of old Japanese furniture are bought and sold at antique shops in America for outrageous prices. Japanese should start taking care of "grandmother's chest of drawers."

What I find difficult when invited to an American home is where to put my glass. Drinks are served before sitting at the table. And I hesitate to put a glass on any of the pieces of furniture because they are all polished to perfection. The kitchen is also kept very clean in American houses. Wives avoid the kind of cooking that may make a mess in the kitchen, such as frying. Americans use the microwave oven all the time. All they need to do is to put in the frozen food they bought at the supermarket and heat it up. Supermarkets carry all sorts of TV dinners. For instance, some chicken, rice, and vegetables are packed in a plastic container. All you need to do is to heat it up in a microwave oven for a few minutes. When ready, you eat it in front of the television. It is that easy. The TV dinner is symbolic of the fast-paced life of this modern age.

Japanese people grill fish, not minding the smell it creates, eat the popular Korean pickle, *kim-chi*, ignoring the aroma of the garlic, and treat their furniture roughly because they do not intend to show it off to others. Americans polish their furniture, keep their kitchens sparkling and odorless, and invite guests in to show off their houses. I am not trying to say which practice is better; I simply find this contrast very interesting.

A Japanese woman staying with an American family in Washington once complained to me, "I put a filet of salmon in a microwave and the wife dashed into the kitchen and opened every single window there. How I wish I could eat fish!" Come to think of it, she looked a little thinner than before.

Randoseru (Ransel)

My American colleague and I wandered into Mitsukoshi Department Store in Nihonbashi, Tokyo, and saw a lot of *randoseru* (backpacks for school books) there. I explained to my colleague, "They are called *randoseru*. Parents and relatives take great pride in giving them to children who have just reached school age."

The colleague I was with in Tokyo was Leigh Hollywood, Vice President of MIGA. When I interviewed him for the position of vice president, I asked him, feeling sure that his answer would be negative, if his last name had anything to do with Hollywood, California, and he replied, "It happens to be my birthplace." Ever since then, whenever I introduce Leigh to Japanese, I make it a rule to say, "This is Mr. Hollywood who was born in Hollywood." Then they remember his name.

I pronounced the word *randoseru* slowly and carefully, thinking that it was probably not an English word. When words of foreign origin with the sound of "r" or "l" are written in *katakana* (the square form of *kana*—the Japanese syllabary), it is not easy to identify between an "l" or "r." So I try first with an "r" and then with an "l." In English "l" and "r" are completely different sounds. I remember feeling like crying when people just kept shaking their heads as I inquired about a subway station on Wall Street. The name of the station was Rector and I was pronouncing it Lector with an "l" instead of an "r." The difference was so slight, but no one understood me. I was indignant at the slow perception of Americans, forgetting my own erroneous pronunciation of the English word. The word rice is with an "r," and if it is not pronounced with the tongue curled upward, it will mean something completely different.

There is an extremely useful dictionary called *The Etymology of Words of Foreign Origin* (Tokyo: Kadokawa). According to this dictionary: "*randoseru*—Dutch, *ransel*, pronounced either [rænsəl] or [rænzəl], *randoseru* is a Japanese transformation." Choei Takano* introduced it in 1950 as *rantosuru*, and it was

*Choei Takano: one of the leading scholars of Western studies, 1804–50

used to store clothes and other things. The present kind, which was designed based on the knapsacks used by the army, was initially used by Gakushuin students in the late Meiji era, then became popular among primary schoolchildren in the cities in the late Taisho era and finally came into general use in the Showa era.

"The *randoseru* is an indispensable object in Japan which gives poetic charm to spring," I explained to Leigh Hollywood, but I don't think he understood. April means spring, cherry blossoms, entrance into school, and *randoseru*. It is a joy to always find something that gives a sense of the seasons when I go back to Japan.

I entered primary school in 1938. The photograph taken on that occasion shows only four or five children in kimonos. But I think everyone had a *randoseru*. Mine was a brown leather one that was a present from my aunt in Amanuma, Tokyo. I was a skinny kid then, and the *randoseru* was thicker than my body. Until third grade, I did not have much to carry in it, and the things in the *randoseru*, notebooks, textbooks, and pencils, made rattling noises when I ran. When I was a fourth grader and had more books and notebooks to fill the *randoseru*, Japan attacked Pearl Harbor. Although the war ended when I was in my second year of junior high school, the postwar period without enough to eat followed. The war lasted for four years and the aftermath was simply miserable. The Gulf War may bring the same sort of aftermath.

Mr. Masaru Ibuka, the founder of Sony, has been giving *randoseru* to employees' children for over 40 years now. When the children reach school age they are invited along with their parents to the head office in Tokyo, all travel expenses paid by the company. In the auditorium of the Sony head office, Mr. Ibuka himself hands a *randoseru* to each child. When I tell American business executives this story they express their admiration frankly, "That's remarkable." Everyone likes to know that someone cares about them. It must be the ultimate delight for parents that the founder of the company gives *randoseru* to their children. They feel that the Sony executives care not only about the employees but about their children as well. This kind of practice is unheard of in America. I can very well understand why American business executives are impressed by it.

On Sunday, February 17, Narita Airport was unusally empty. In the first-class section of my flight there were more flight attendants than passengers, Thinking, "It's a perfect day for playing golf," I departed from Narita with much reluctance. I arrived at Dulles Airport in Washington after a 12-hour flight to find a cold, wintery Sunday there.

Back in my apartment I could not tell if I was sleepy or not, but I lay down and slept soundly until the telephone woke me up. It was still light outside. It was my secretary Celia. I said abruptly, "What time is it now?" and she told me it was five o'clock in the afternoon.

After she gave me her message, she added that the brown-bag meeting the other day had been very favorably commented upon by MIGA staff. At present (1991) MIGA has 55 staff members from 22 different countries. Every Wednesday afternoon at 12:30 they gather in a meeting room, each carrying a brown bag with their favorite food and drinks. We call it a brown-bag meeting. And for one hour they talk about whatever they fancy. I am always a listener. At a brown-bag meeting you can have your say and also hear what others are thinking. Meetings of this sort are essential for an international organization like MIGA. Maybe I will talk about *randoseru* at the next brown-bag meeting.

A Corduroy Suit

My cousin's eldest son came to Washington rather unexpectedly.

He sent me a fax only a few days before, saying that he was coming, and then there he was. It was his first visit to the East Coast. His name is Koichi and he is 39 years old.

I took him to a French restaurant called Maison Blanche. It means "white house" in French, and it is in fact located near the White House. He had a beige corduroy suit on, and looked very clean, despite the fact that he had arrived in Washington only three hours earlier. After ordering in fluent English, he remarked, looking at the patrons there, "It looks as if the American establishment is here." I had been feeling uneasy and I was wondering what caused this disquiet. Then I realized that it was because Koichi looked fully acclimatized to the surroundings of Washington. He never showed any excitement or amazement, saying things like "Washington is so pretty," "The whole town looks like a park," or "It's so spacious and open, and so different from Tokyo."

It was 36 years ago when I first came to America. I arrived in Seattle from Yokohama after a 14-day voyage, and I was impressed by every single thing I saw. Everything was so different. Everything was a surprise for me, even the discovery that uniformed laborers on the wharf and beggars on the street were all white was a surprise. The first Americans I had encountered were GIs stationed in Japan—heavily built, healthy looking military men clad in well-tailored uniforms made from fine quality material strode the streets of Tokyo. That effect can best be described as "the relationship between the winners and the losers of the war." But I was surprised, when I saw America with my own eyes, to find that there were different kinds of people among the winners.

Surprises continued. The dormitory of the University of Pennsylvania was heated, you could walk around naked after taking a hot, gushing shower while snow silently fell on the ground. It was paradise. Milk was incredibly rich, hot dogs were enormous. My roommates, Tom and George, were both football players over 1.9 meters (6 feet 3 inches) tall with firm muscular bodies. The "things" dangling in front of their bodies were also long and big, and I remember feeling hopelessly miserable every time I saw them.

In 1853 Commodore Perry came to Uraga with four "black ships." The shogunate government consulted the daimyo (feudal lords) as to whether the country should be opened to the world. Public opinion was split into two. Perry came again the following year, the Japan-U.S. Peace Treaty was concluded, and in 1856 Townsend Harris arrived in Shimoda as the first consul-general from the U.S. to Japan.

Some scholars say U.S.-Japan relations were forced upon Japan by the U.S., i.e., that it was not a normal relationship from the beginning. I do not know enough history to comment on this matter, but I imagine the difference between Japan and the U.S. at that time must have been far greater in many ways than now.

In 1860 Masaomi Niimi came to America to ratify the Treaty. Kaishu Katsu also came on the *Kanrin-maru*. Samurai with double swords received a hearty welcome from Americans in San Francisco, Washington, D.C., and New York. I wonder what those samurai thought of America. There are many publications dealing with the event. According to them, the astonishment the samurai experienced when they came to America was much greater than mine. That is not really surprising, but I always find it amusing to read about their experiences.

Takashi Muragaki, the great-grandson of the governor of Awaji, Norimasa Muragaki, a member of the first delegation, works in the World Bank in Washington, D.C. The Japanese Embassy in Washington has a framed photograph of the delegation, and Takashi Muragaki looks very much like his great-grandfather in the photograph. He and I often play golf together, and whenever I praise him by shouting, "Nice shot, Governor of Awaji!" he loses his composure and his shots become inaccurate.

Different generations seem to have different opinions of U.S.-Japan relations. I have a fixed idea that the U.S. is wealthy and powerful. I cannot say it out loud, but somewhere in my heart I have something like a sense of defeat, and feel that we are powerless against the U.S. People of my generation, who belong neither to the war generation nor to the postwar generation, who, although I do not like the expression, belong to the generation of war damage and destruction, have opinions of the U.S. that are fundamentally different from those of young people. *Amerika Hijiki* (American Seaweed) by Akiyuki Nosaka very well describes our generation's feeling toward the U.S.

Even among people of the same generation there are pro-American and anti-American people, and that is inevitable. However, I cannot help thinking that, regardless of their pro- or anti-American feelings, people of my generation have deep in their hearts the same fixed idea of the U.S. Ever since the breakout of the Gulf War, the U.S. soldiers in Saudi Arabia are often shown on television. Although camouflage uniform is not very familiar to Japanese, when I see their faces in close-up they overlap with the image of the GIs I used to see after World War II. In particular, the Chief of Staff's expressions and posture at the Pentagon press conference were exactly the same as the officers of World War II. Americans in their mid-60s do not seem to look at the Gulf War without thinking of World War II. Just yesterday, in commentary on CNN, a retired general explained in detail, using the film of the battle of Iwojima for emphasis, the terror to be expected when the ground fighting begins. I watched it with mixed feelings.

Koichi spent three days in Washington. Dressed casually in jeans and sneakers, he left on a non-stop flight to Tokyo, his face expressionless as ever.

The Young

I sometimes receive telephone calls from strangers. Most of the strangers who call me are Japanese graduate students studying in the U.S. And almost always the purpose of the call is to seek help or advice in their job hunting. They beg me to spare time for them, so I suggest, "Would you like to come on xx day at xx time?" And they say "Well, that is not very convenient." So I do my best to find some other time, and I make another proposal, but that is not convenient for them either. Naturally I wonder why I have to accommodate their schedules, but I tell myself "Patience, patience." I try to see these young people even for only five or ten minutes, because I am interested in knowing what they are thinking about.

Yesterday five university students from Japan came, led by Mr. Ibe of Nichibei Kaiwa Gakuin. Mr. Ibe's father, Mr. Masaichi Ibe, was a professor at Waseda when I was a student there. He often gave lectures at his home near Hatoyama Palace in Otowa. Mr. Ibe, the son, was a toddler then, but he must be nearly 40 now. To my grief, Professor Ibe passed away in 1976.

Mr. Mikio Kanda, who is also a Waseda graduate, founded the Japan-U.S. Culture Center in Washington, D.C., which has been putting on various cultural events over the years. A speech contest was held in 1991 in Tokyo and part of the prize was a round-trip air ticket from Tokyo to Washington. Nichibei Kaiwa Gakuin took part in this program and that was why Mr. Ibe came to Washington with the five students, the winners of the speech contest. There were three boys from Kitakyushu, Tohoku, and Waseda universities, and two girls from Tsuda and Keio universities.

I showed the six of them into the small conference room where our executive staff meeting is held every Monday. The room seats eight people comfortably, but as I was briefing them on the World Bank and MIGA, I began to feel oppressed by their youthful intensity, and intimidated by their piercing eyes focused on me. We moved to a larger room in the middle of the meeting.

Mr. Ibe asked me to say a word to the students. This is where I feel most awkward. It gives me an inferiority complex to find that the others are often more knowledgeable or have deeper insight. The five students were staring at me like chicks waiting, with their mouths open, to be fed by their mother. I had no choice but to project myself and say whatever was on my mind. I told them stories of my many failures, starting with what a chaotic and decadent life I had led when I was their age.

"My major is English literature. English is very important, in fact it is everything for me. These other four are majoring in economics or law, and English is only secondary for them. Tell me, what do you think of English?" the Kitakyushu boy asked sticking his lips out. He had a bad case of acne on his lip and it looked painful.

I am often asked what I think of English. This is what I think: You must be aware of the very plain fact that no matter how proficient you become in English, you will never be able to say more in English than you can say in your own language. In other words, although you need to have ability to express yourself in English, what is more important is the substance you want to express. I often feel discouraged by my inability to express myself, as well as by the poor substance of my remarks.

It is often said that although Japanese are not very good at speaking or comprehending English, they are good at reading and writing it, but I do not agree. It should rather be said that Japanese are poor at speaking, comprehending, reading, and writing English, but they can do a little better in reading and writing than in speaking and comprehending. Intellectuals of the Meiji era could indeed read English. They had no choice but to study the original texts. Nowadays translations come out so quickly that the Japanese do not read English very much any more, and consequently their reading ability has declined.

No one will ever be able to speak English like an American unless born and educated in America. If you come to America as an adult, you will have to struggle with English for the rest of your life.

The best way to improve your English is to increase your vocabulary. You need at least 10,000 words. And even if you know 10,000 words, you will be only using 2,000 words at the most when you speak or write, although you will understand the rest when you read or hear them.

"I would like to do something to contribute to the development of the world economy, sharing life with people in the third world, rather than working in an international organization like the World Bank or the United Nations," the Tohoku boy spoke clearly, looking at me through his fashionable round glasses. "I would like to work for an international organization," said the Keio girl, with flushed cheeks and straight white teeth that could be used for a toothpaste commercial. "I still don't know what I want to do," the Tsuda girl said, bending her head so deeply that her long hair covered her face. The sleepy-looking Waseda boy remained silent throughout the meeting.

Cherry Blossoms by the Potomac River

On television I saw a gentleman, neatly dressed in a suit, looking painstakingly at three cherry trees in the Yasukuni Shrine in Kudan. He was a meteorologist and was deciding when to announce the blossoming of the cherry trees. The buds had not even expanded to the stipulated level and he had to leave without making any decision. The next day, on March 30, the opening of the cherry blossoms was finally announced. It was ten days later than the previous year.

I left Narita on the All Nippon Airways flight for Washington and arrived at Washington Dulles Airport on the same day.

Although it was a little chilly with the temperature reaching only 10°C (50°F), it was a fine day. It took me about 40 minutes by car from the airport to Washington. Because it was Sunday the traffic was light.

There is an inlet on the Potomac River, by the Jefferson Memorial, forming a pond called the Tidal Basin, along the banks of which are many cherry trees. Eighty years ago, Tokyo Mayor Yukio Ozaki donated these trees on the occasion of the inauguration of President Taft. With one such act, a person can be remembered forever.

Washington's cherry blossoms are at their best now. In one week, the cherry blossom festival is to take place. Among various events is a Miss Japanese-American contest. When the Gulf War broke out, it was feared that the festival might not be possible, but fortunately the war did not prevent it from taking place as scheduled.

A thirty-minute drive from Washington takes you to a residential area in Maryland called Kenwood. The cherry blossoms there are breathtaking. Kenwood seems to me a very affluent residential area, but by American standards it belongs only to the upper middle-class level. Every house is built on the spacious area of at least half an acre. There is a regulation in the neighborhood that they have to have a certain number of cherry trees. Some are more than one meter in diameter, and more than 50 years old. When the blossoms open everywhere, one no longer sees the sky. The mass of pink and white is overwhelming.

Americans do not enjoy themselves drinking and singing, sitting on a mat, beneath the cherry trees. Americans love parties, but they do not have them under the cherry trees, appreciating the blossoms. Japanese have a strong passion for cherry blossoms, and their aesthetic sense never fails to praise the beauty of blossoms when they are about to fall. There is a part of the doctrine of Japanese chivalry which declares that the business of the samurai is to die. Therefore, the falling cherry blossoms can be seen as a synonym for men falling. They also recall the military badge during World War II. And if you let your mind flow that far, cherry blossoms bring bitter memories to people like me who were born in the 1920s and 1930s. Cherry blossoms have different meanings for people of different ages and situations.

Young people may not believe it, but there was a time when Sokeisen (Waseda-Keio) baseball was almost a national event like the Nihon Series of today. I suppose this was until about 1955. In the outfield bleachers of Waseda, a seven- or eight-meter-long streamer, with the words "Blossom of cherry, men of Waseda" written in large letters, carried by the students, was waved back and forth regardless of winning or losing.

Americans do not seem to appreciate the night view of the cherry blossoms. "The blossoms were so spectacular in the daylight, but when we went back at night it was too dark to see," say many disappointed Japanese tourists. In America there is no custom of enjoying the blossoms at night, so they do not put out lights. Cherry blossoms in Japan are displayed remarkably by illumination, which can be either from the bottom of the trees skyward or by lanterns in the branches.

"Cherry blossoms at night . . . crows cawing in the moonlight . . . someone is hiding behind the tree . . . don't pretend . . . willows with buds swing gently in the breeze . . ." The night sky is the symbol of Yoshiwara.* "Going to view cherry blossoms at night" is said to have been argot for "going to Yoshiwara." The above is a lilting song about frequenters of the gay quarters. Unusually, my Kouta (ditty) instructor taught me this song at the very beginning. I was later told that generally they start with an easier piece. It was not easy to learn and that is why I have a special attachment to the song.

I think it was about ten years ago when I went to see the cherry blossoms in Tokyo's Shiba Park at night. For some reason there

---

*Yoshiwara: former red-light district of old Tokyo

were not many people there. I think the lights there were lanterns, since I could see the petals clearly. Sometimes I miss the sense of the seasons that you can feel when living in Japan. I experience this syndrome especially when returning to America from a short visit to Japan. I do not mean that there is no sense of the seasons in American life. Different nations have a different rhythm of life. Maybe the problem lies in my attitude toward life. No matter how long I live in America I still feel that I am only a visitor, and that some day I will be going back to Japan. I am afraid I will be caught in this dilemma for quite some time.

A Dog in Georgetown

I am not particularly fond of dogs. Neither do I dislike them. I feel rather neutral about them. On an unseasonably warm Sunday in mid-April, with the temperature reaching 85° F, so warm that young people were out on the river bank sun-bathing, I saw a man walking a Boston terrier along the street in Georgetown, an affluent residential area of Washington that has an 18th-century air. He was a tall thin man with dark sunglasses and clear-cut features that looked Indian or Pakistani. I spoke to him, "It's a Boston terrier, isn't it? I used to have one myself." "He is blind in one eye, and completely deaf," the man said in a deep voice. Boston terriers are small dogs with features similar to that of a boxer. They have white hair around the nose and between the eyes, but otherwise are black, which makes them look as if they are in a tuxedo.

Nearly thirty years ago, when my wife was in low spirits after her first pregnancy ended in a miscarriage, our American friend who lived in Denenchofu* gave her a puppy to cheer her up. My wife, for whom dogs were always a part of life, was delighted and

*Denenchofu: an expensive residential district in southwest Tokyo

looked after it as if it were her own child. And that puppy was a Boston terrier. She named it Pero because he liked to lick—*"pero, pero"* in Japanese—with his rough tongue. We later found out that *pero* also means "dog" in Spanish. A trainer came every day for six months to train Pero. In the hallway of the apartment, the dog would push a wooden toy cart back and forth with his front paws. The cart contained several rabbits which alternately rose and fell as the cart was pushed. He slept by my wife's feet and when I sneaked up to bed, coming home late and drunk, he would growl at me. If I came too near, he would dash toward me as if to bite me in the throat. There was only one mistress for him in the whole wide world: my wife. The loyal servant showed by his action his mistress's grudge against her drunken husband who often did not come home until after midnight. Pero lived for ten years and died of old age in New York.

My second oldest daughter, Haruko, had a Pekinese when she lived alone in New York. His name was Pooh. He was a cuddly thing with a lot of soft fluffy hair, but he was temperamental and would bite when angered. He was frustrated because he was not taken out to walk. Walking is as indispensable for dogs as eating. Haruko occasionally phoned me from New York, "May I come down to Washington this weekend with Pooh?" "You can't bring Pooh." Then Haruko would protest, "But Pooh loves you." Once when I visited her New York apartment, Pooh pushed his nose out of the door and trotted toward me as I got off the elevator. Since then Haruko decided that Pooh loved me. Haruko is leaving for Japan tomorrow for good, along with Pooh.

About ten years ago, my eldest daughter Akiko, then a junior high-school student, brought home a stray kitten she found in the corner of the schoolyard. It was a tortoise-shell. "Her name is Inuko (*inu*=dog, *ko*=child; little)."

"But why? She is a cat."

"Right. My friends and I decided to call her Inuko," Akiko said as if there was nothing unusual about it. When the cat was missing, she would look for it crying, "Inuko!, Inuko!" A neighbor asked, "Is your dog missing?" She started at me quizzically when I said, "No, it is our cat that is missing." Inuko was later adopted by our close friend, and grew to be a beautiful cat. Her owner was a professional photographer and Inuko appeared a number of times in the NHK (Japan Broadcasting Corporation) course entitled "How to Photograph Your Pets."

My son Seido one day picked up a big black cat that had a mean-looking face. As he was found in a school in Hiyoshi, we named him "Hiyoshi." Despite his appearance, he was a friendly cat and liked to snuggle up. One stormy night Hiyoshi vanished. Our third eldest daughter, Kuniko, who adored Hiyoshi, drove around the neighborhood looking for him, and found him crouching for shelter in front of the display window of a clothing shop about a mile away from home.

In the house in Kichijoji, my family now has four dogs and three cats. When I go home I occasionally take the dogs out for a walk. I put on my gloves and take a small shovel, a newspaper, and a paper bag. When they do their business I scoop it up with the shovel, wrap it in the newspaper, and put it in the paper bag.

When you walk on the streets in Georgetown, you can step on dogs' droppings if you are not careful. There are many ill-mannered dog-owners who take their dogs out for a walk without taking a shovel, newspaper, and a paper bag.

Oxbridge

Every night before going to bed I debate whether or not I should chain the door, and I always end up chaining it. Then the ominous thought crosses my mind that if I have a heart attack during the night, even if a doctor hastens to my apartment, he will not be able to come in if the door is chained. I have had this fear for the last two or three years. It is not that I am in poor physical condition. I suppose it is my age.

My wife sometimes comes to visit me from Tokyo, but normally I live alone. It is not new to me, since I lived alone in New York for three years. Once you get used to living alone, and set your own pace of life, it is not as hard as it may appear. However, when you live alone in America, you must be careful how other people look at you. It is customary to attend all kinds of evening functions, such as receptions and dinner parties, as a couple, and if a married man shows up alone, it appears odd.

My secretary Celia once whispered to me in a low voice, "When I applied for a job in MIGA, I was warned, 'Be aware that the man who will be your boss keeps saying that his wife is coming from Tokyo to join him, but she never seems to arrive.' " I was amused more by her manner, which I thought was very much like a Japanese, than the story itself. It is only in Japan that it is common to proceed to a new post leaving the family behind. In the rest of the world this is something unheard of.

It does not happen very often, but sometimes people question me persistently about my wife's absence. I know they do not mean to make me feel uncomfortable. They simply cannot comprehend why I am here alone, and they look dubiuosly at me as if I am an alien from another planet. Since I know that no explanation can convince these people, I simply smile at them when they ask me the question, and try to bear the momentary discomfort this causes me. I remain silent because I know I will be attacked with a wave of counterarguments once I open my mouth. Soon someone will change the subject.

There are two kinds of men both in America and in Japan: one is the kind who starts talking about his family only a few minutes after meeting someone for the first time, and the other is the kind who never says anything about his family unless asked. There is a widely believed misconception in Japan that the majority of

American men belong to the former type, because it is said that American men devote themselves to their families rather than to their companies, but the truth is that the majority of WASPs belong to the latter type. They seem to abide strictly by the rule that they should not touch on personal matters except with close acquaintances. And also they are a little bit shy. Japanese men are considered to belong to the latter type because they put top priority on their work, neglecting their families. This may be true about men over 60. But surprisingly many men seem to take pleasure in talking about their wives and children, when no-one appears to be particularly interested in hearing. Perhaps they do that because they have happy families. The trouble is that they lack the sensitivity to remember that not everyone is as lucky as they are. Perhaps they are not considerate enough to think about it.

Some people like to talk about their alma mater and others do not. You rarely hear Americans say the name of the school they went to. They would refer to their school indirectly, "When I was in school in Boston . . . " Almost always those who talk like that are Harvard graduates, even though there are many other universities in Boston such as MIT and Boston University. In Japan, University of Tokyo graduates used to say, "When I was in Hongo . . . " Hongo suggests Akamon,* which in turn suggests Todai.* But that manner of speech is not prevalent any more.

An hour's talk will enable you to tell those who went to Keio, Hitotsubashi, or Kyoto University. It is not that there are stereotypes, but they drop hints about their alma mater. I presume they are strongly attached to their school, are proud of it, and have a strong bond between classmates. In contrast, Tokyo or Waseda graduates cannot be easily identified.

---

*Akamon: famous red gateway of the University of Tokyo

*Todai: popular abbreviation for the University of Tokyo

Many of the World Bank and IMF staff are Oxbridge (Oxford and Cambridge) graduates. Among them, aside from the British, are many Indians, Pakistanis, Canadians and other nationals. And many of them hold Ph.Ds.

After World War II, Japan adopted the American education system, and so far has done quite well with it. But now the U.S., the originator of this education system, is further expanding its graduate schools in an attempt to bring back to school those who are already at work. Law schools and business schools are good examples. Only the Japanese stop studying completely at the early age of 23, thinking they can let their minds lie fallow thanks to the lifetime employment they enter once they graduate from a prestigious school, and immerse themselves in the competitive business world.

I have the feeling that within a few years there will be more graduate schools in Japan for teaching practical business and law.

Foggy Bottom Station

The face looked familiar but I could not remember who she was. A tall, oriental woman was gazing intently at the wall map at the Foggy Bottom metro station. She wore no make-up and her hair was drawn back, and with her fair complexion she looked about 40 years old. I had a feeling that she was someone I knew fairly well rather than someone I saw somewhere once before.

The area from the Kennedy Center on the bank of the Potomac River to George Washington University is called Foggy Bottom. The bottom of the earth veiled in the river mist . . . I always thought it was such a romantic name. But a Washingtonian told me that I was totally mistaken. "This area was named Foggy Bottom by some sarcastic people because it used to be crowded with glass factories and the air was always dusty with smoke, which looked like fog from a distance."

The majority of the passengers who use Foggy Bottom station are George Washington University students or government workers. The oriental woman was still standing there.

I became impatient and could not resist speaking to her, "Er, excuse me." She turned to me with a start. "I am glad you approached me. I was hesitating to speak to you," she said delightedly. There was a small mole at the left corner of her mouth.

Dusk was drawing near. The large red sun was setting to the west of Pennsylvania Avenue. The sky was suffused with red as if in flames. I still could not remember who she was. Our long shadows were cast over the brick sidewalk as we walked side by side. The spring evening air, which was neither too warm nor too cold, gently embraced us. The woman said, "What a fortunate chance," as she picked at her tiramisu with a fork at the Italian restaurant Donatello. She had such a beautiful voice. In the candlelight I saw some charming lines at the corners of her eyes. Later we would go to Washington Harbor and when we came to be in romantic mood, enveloped in the gentle breeze blowing from the river, we would stroll hand in hand, humming a tune.

Here I am again daydreaming, letting my imagination roam endlessly. The oriental woman, still standing in front of the map, gave a deep sigh. Suddenly she turned toward me. I saw her full-face, but did not recognize her. Her eyes were not focused on me very long. Her expression did not change in the slightest. Then she began to walk briskly away. I was mistaken after all. I quickened my pace and hastened back to my Watergate apartment. It is less than five minutes walk from the metro station.

Because homeless people hang about the station, one more guard was added to the previous two. I saw a white man wrapped in a colorful blanket, despite the warm temperature, walking slowly toward me. Since his face was covered with a beard I could not tell his age. I gave him a dollar bill when he held his hand out to me. "God bless you," he said clearly.

During the Gulf War I often watched President Bush deliver speeches on television, and at the close of each speech he said "God bless you." I wonder how to translate that phrase into Japanese any other way than "Mercy of God upon you."

As soon as I got home I took a shower and shaved. I put on my tuxedo, and as I left the building, Mary, the receptionist, a plump woman in her 50s, who used to live in Yokohama, said "You look nice."

A dinner party hosted by the International Automobile Manufacturers Association was in progress at the Four Seasons Hotel in Georgetown. The guests, men in tuxedos and ladies in backless evening gowns, were predominantly middle-aged Caucasians.

Mrs. Smith, who sat next to me, was a very talkative woman. She began to lose her voice as a result of having to shout in order to be heard in the noisy room. Despite that, she still kept on talking. "My son is 20 years old and a junior in the university. He is determined to become a drug investigator. He is over six feet tall and is very good at Karate, so he works as a guard on the campus. Drug investigator is a very dangerous occupation, isn't it? I am definitely against it, but he doesn't listen to me. He is such a stubborn boy." It is indeed a dangerous occupation. Almost every day murders are committed in Washington, and most of the murder cases are drug-related. Drug traffickers do not hesitate to pull a gun. Every year some policemen are killed too.

I thought this was too heavy a topic for conversation with someone your are meeting for the first time and in such noisy surroundings. "Your son must be a very upright person," I said, trying to divert the conversation. "Upright? On the contrary. He was on drugs himself. Maybe that's why he doesn't want anyone else to experience the agony he had to go through."

Fireflies

Washington's summer is notorious for its high temperature and humidity. Even so, it is not normal for the temperature to be near 100°F (38°C) for several days in succession in May. The moment you step out of doors, the hot and humid air stops your brain from functioning and you have to concentrate on walking, paying full attention to avoid being hit by a car. It is so hazy that the Capitol and the Washington Monument look blurred, as if in a mirage. I could accept the warm weather if it were midsummer, but the fact that it is only May, which is supposed to be the best time of the year, annoys me and makes the high temperature even more intolerable.

Besides, I have not been feeling well. It has been a hectic month. Starting in late April I had to travel to Vancouver, New York, Oakland, Tokyo, Izumo, Sano, and Toronto. I had a throat problem and a difficulty in speaking while in Tokyo, and my wife made me go to see an ear, nose, and throat specialist in Kichijoji. "Open your mouth and say 'a-a-a-h'. There's no need to be so nervous." The doctor was as swaggering as the one I used to see when I was little. He touched the tender part of my throat with a metal stick with medicine on the tip. I felt a burning pain. I remembered that my mother used to say that you will be cured in a minute if you have your doctor burn your throat.

A young nurse in white took me to an inhalator in the corner of the room. As a little boy I used to have to wear a bib and inhale vapor with my mouth wide open. "Your vocal cords are badly swollen. Try not to speak," I was informed solemnly. I walked through the wooden hallway making shuffling noises with the slippers I had been given, and left the clinic, which smelled of cresol. I felt nostalgic, as if I had gone back 50 years through a time machine.

I did not think much about my throat but soon I began to cough so violently that my body was wracked with pain. Despite my illness I had to return to Washington on the All Nippon Airways flight as scheduled. When I arrived at my Watergate apartment, I took two aspirins with a large glass of fresh orange juice. The best remedy for a cold is some aspirin, orange juice, and a good sleep—following American doctors' advice I crawled into bed and closed my eyes. I slept soundly for 15 hours. No, my sleep was not sound. I had many dreams. I got up and took another dose of aspirin and orange juice. I was beginning to feel better. The clock read 7:00 in the morning. My hip ached as a result of sleeping too long. I had a slight fear that maybe I was taking a risk but said to myself 'I will cross that bridge when I come to it,' and rushed to the health club and jumped into the swimming pool. The cold water felt invigorating on my skin. I swam 30 laps (60 lengths) of breast stroke in a 15-meter swimming pool. There was no one else there.

I thought of going to work. I checked my diary and found that I had nothing scheduled for that day, which was unusual. I phoned my secretary Celia to ask her to send round to my apartment the documents that needed to be read through that day, and told her that I would not be coming in because I had a cold. Celia called me back and asked who I wished to deputize in my absence. That is where the international organizations differ from private companies. Where responsibility and authority lie should be specified at all times in an organization like the World Bank. Having answered, "Mr. Hollywood," I went back to bed and slept again. I could sleep endlessly as if I were a young person again. I wondered what was wrong with me.

It was five o'clock when I woke up. I felt better. I decided that golf would be the best solution for fatigue and jet lag, and called Mr. Kikuchi of the World Bank, who, fortunately, was still in the office. He agreed to go to play golf with me, and came to pick me up at 5:30. It was still muggy outside. Mr. Kikuchi drives fast and we were at a country club called Bretton Woods in 40 minutes. Bretton Woods is actually the name of a New Hampshire town.

The foundation of the World Bank and IMF was determined at the international conference held there in 1944. Hence, the World Bank and IMF are called Bretton Woods Organizations. The country club is owned by the IMF, and its members are IMF and World Bank staff. Woodlands are scattered over an extensive plain, through which the green fairways of the golf course meander.

We teed off at 6:30 and finished half the round at eight. It was still light. "My wife will have dinner prepared," Mr. Kikuchi invited me over to his home. The residential area of Bethesda looks like Karuizawa, one of Japan's wooded resort areas, and Mr. Kikuchi's elegant house is surrounded by plane trees, dogwoods, oaks, and maples. Emiko, Mr. Kikuchi's wife, greeted me at the door. She is a professional painter who paints patterns on kimonos. She also writes "News from Washington" for a Japanese weekly magazine, and occasionally she asks me to look through her manuscript. It is not my place to criticize other people's writings. Besides, her style is very fresh and I envy her sensitivity.

Inari-zushi (fried bean curd stuffed with seasoned rice), *gyoza* (Chinese-style fried dumplings), *hiya-yakko* (cold bean curd), and *negi-nuta* (scallions with soy bean paste)—my favorite foods, were placed on the table. Their ten-year-old daughter, Rema, was still up to keep us company at a late dinner at nearly 10 o'clock. Rema stood up and went to the porch saying "I am going to catch fireflies." Mrs. Kikuchi said, pointing to their garden, "We already have lots of fireflies around here." It was so quiet, not a sound could be heard.

Birthday Party

"Until only three years ago these skirts and dresses fitted me perfectly . . ." sighed Celia, my secretary, and gave Toni, the receptionist, the clothes that no longer fitted her. Toni said "Are you sure I can have all these?" but accepted them happily. Today is Toni's twenty-sixth birthday. Celia has been busy preparing since this morning, and looking at her memo pad she is mumbling, "He is taking care of the champagne, she will be bringing a cake."

Celia looks slimmer than she seems to think. She is certainly bigger than Toni, but for her age—mid-40s—she is in good shape. She goes to her neighborhood sports club from 6:00 AM to 7:30 AM and does aerobics before coming to work. For lunch she only eats some cooked vegetables and iced tea. I do not understand why she has to worry so much about her figure just because she cannot wear her old skirts, but it seems to disturb her tremendously. "Why don't you get some new skirts?" I said to her. "I don't have that kind of money," she said—and she looked offended.

It is not wise to get yourself involved in women's talk about figures. If a woman says "I have gained weight," you can reply "Yes, you have," "No, you haven't," or just remain silent. Perhaps the last is the best solution. They are not actually seeking any answer from men. In a way, it is a soliloquy, so it's better not to pay any attention.

Today's birthday party starts at 4:00 PM. Finally, I am beginning to understand the system of parties in the World Bank. I used to be reluctant to have parties in the office during working hours. In Nomura Securities where I used to work, the period from 8:40 AM to 5:00 PM was sacred and inviolable "working hours." During those hours you had to work to the best of your ability, dealing with clients or watching exchange rates that kept changing constantly. Meetings in the office, such as staff meetings in the morning or strategy meetings in the evening, were held outside the working hours. Early morning meetings would start at 8:00 AM and evening meetings did not start until 6:00 PM. It was an unthinkable idea to have a birthday party in the office in the middle of the day, and no-one even considered such a thing.

Right at 4:00 PM, Jeremy, a Nigerian economist in his mid 30s, came in and held his hand out. I said "Welcome" and shook his hand. He held my hand so hard it hurt terribly. "Jeremy, you must be careful. You really shouldn't squeeze so hard." He shook my hand again, "Then, like this?" He held it softly, and it gave me an eerie feeling. By 5:00 PM, my office was filled with about 40 people. Toni, the birthday girl, was so excited that she could not sit still. Celia said, "Everybody, attention please," and started singing, in a professional operatic voice, "Happy birthday to you . . ." Everybody followed—women's voices, men's voices, high and low, husky and clear. There were ten small candles on a chocolate-frosted, 12-inch birthday cake. I put the cake slowly on the desk so as not to let the quivering flames be blown out. Toni's delicate face lit by the candles shone brightly. She blew out all the candles. Everybody clapped.

Then, a stocky man came in. It was John from Colombia who works in the research division. He has a very prominent nose and there are three deep horizontal lines on his forehead under a receding hairline. Celia poured champagne for him, and he said, "Thank you. Today is Toni's birthday, but I got married yesterday." Everybody was stunned, and silence prevailed in the room.

John emptied his glass and started talking quietly: his wife had passed away a few years ago. He met a woman who lived in the neighborhood. Both of them are in their mid-50s. They each have two college-age children. He continued, "I am sorry I didn't inform you earlier, but when I woke up yesterday morning I realized that I had a day off and thought that the city hall must be less crowded because it was a weekday. I rang my friend and we went to the city hall to register." He said that afterwards they went to an Italian restaurant and celebrated with champagne and spaghetti.

The lines on his forehead began to fill with perspiration as he went on speaking. I felt an urge to wipe it with my handkerchief but I refrained. "Congratulations, John!" I toasted, and everybody followed. The party ended exactly at 6:00 PM.

Girard's Law

Living overseas, you often have to entertain visitors from Japan by taking them to restaurants and showing them around. Sometimes you need only have one meal with them, but on other occasions you have to be with them for breakfast, lunch, and dinner for two or three days. Some Japanese residing in America complain that it is a complete waste of time and energy to entertain visitors from Japan. I, on the contrary, enjoy entertaining them. There are not many opportunities to meet and spend time with famous or accomplished people whom you may never otherwise see, or people whose style of life is completely different. There is a saying in Japan *"Ichigo, ichie,"* (Every meeting happens only once.) It is a phrase used in the tea ceremony, and it means "Every occasion of extending hospitality to another person is a particular occasion never to recur again in one's lifetime (so one should try to make the occasion perfect)."

I sometimes become very close to people with whom I have spent only a few days in New York or Washington, and I feel indescribably lonely when I come home alone after seeing them off at the airport. "I will see you in Tokyo. Do not fail to contact me. I would like to reciprocate the kindness you showed me." They hold my hand firmly. More often than not, I never see these people again. Every meeting happens only once—but I always treasure the memory.

Even extremely busy people who are always pressed for time in Tokyo, constantly looking at their watches, or very famous people whom everyone knows and who are always conscious of other people's eyes, can instantly relax when they go abroad.

Everyone from famous authors, Kabuki actors, movie stars, politicians, and scholars, to pro-golfers, reveals their real selves then. And this makes one glad to be an overseas representative of a Japanese firm.

I like famous people. It makes me feel good to be acquainted with them because then I feel as if I am someone. "You are such a lowbrow," my wife and children say contemptuously. The only consolation is that I know I have not fallen so low as to broadcast the fact that I am acquainted with particular famous people.

There are people who say, as soon as the name of a famous person is mentioned, "Oh, him. I know him very well." And they say this even when they have only exchanged business cards at a party or somewhere. If they have had a dinner together, they will boast, "Oh, him. He is a close friend of mine." I find it more thrilling to remain silent and just smile when the name of a famous person whom I know quite well is mentioned.

There are many levels of associating with people, each described in Japanese by an appropriate saying, from "Every meeting happens only once," or "Even a chance meeting is due to the karma from a previous life," to closer friendship such as a "friendship of fish and water" or the still more intimate "friendship of decapitation." "Friendship of fish and water" refers to intimate friends who are inseparable, like a fish which dies when it leaves the water, and "friendship of decapitation" means devoted, sworn friends, even at the risk of death. This last is the friendship described in Osamu Dazai's *Run, Melos*, and is familiar to Westerners in the ancient Greek tale of Damon and Pythias.

If asked whether I have a bosom friend, I would probably bow my head in shame. Because I haven't. And I am ashamed of myself for my lack of perseverance in not having a bosom friend, though I wish I did.

But I try not to go that deeply into the matter and instead think less seriously about friendship. To be more concrete, where should the linc bc drawn between "friends" and "acquaintances"?

Joe Girard, who was recorded in the Guiness Book of Records as the best car salesman in the world, wrote "Girard's Law of 250 People." Mr. Girard asked a clergyman who had bought a car from him, "How many people come to a funeral service when someone dies?" and the clergyman replied, "About 250 people on average." When I attended a wedding I asked the master of ceremonies the number of guests, and he told me that it was about 250 from the bride's side and the groom's respectively.

Thus, an ordinary person has about 250 relatives and friends. The key to successful selling is to offer the utmost service to your current customers. And if you are lucky, those people will pass the word to friends and relatives, and you will gain 250 more customers. The amount of effort needed to gain an additional 250 customers that way would be about one tenth of what you would need to make to find new customers on your own. That idea flashed upon the king of salesman.

Every summer I think I will make a Christmas card list during my summer holiday and start writing the cards in the fall to give myself plenty of time. Alas, I have not carried it out for the last 30 years. With Americans, as long as you exchange Christmas cards you are considered friends, but once you stop sending Christmas cards, your connections are severed. Hand-written Christmas cards mean a great deal in America. I am afraid my increasing neglect of sending Christmas cards is making me lose my American friends with whom I made so much effort to establish friendships. On the other hand, I do not mind so much if mass-produced printed Christmas cards from companies stop coming.

"What would you do if you are told that you have only one more week to live?" I was suddenly asked by my friend who was also reaching 60, in the middle of the day, when he was not even drunk. "Well, perhaps I would make a list of people to send my death notice to," was my immediate response. I had answered such because the matter of the Christmas card list was just then hanging heavily on my mind.

Goodbye, Celia

Celia was looking up at the clear blue sky, swinging in a hammock beneath the shade of palm trees. She is a mixed beauty in her 40s with Caucasian features and brown skin. "I wonder if I could make a good wife to a Governor." It was not only the hammock that was in motion—so was Celia's heart. She was still in a state of excitement over Peter's words of last night.

Four hours by jet from Washington, D.C., the British Virgin Islands in the Caribbean is a British colony. The Governor sent from Great Britain reigns over 17,000 people just like a king. Celia had arrived the previous day.

Peter Penfold is the Governor. He is a Londoner who went to a school located next to Prime Minister Major's school. As soon as he graduated from university, he passed the diplomatic service examination and began working at the Foreign Office. His first overseas assignment was Trinidad-Tobago in the Caribbean, and the second was Uganda. At the same time, Celia had been sent to Uganda by the World Bank. The political situation in Uganda at that time, five years ago, was extremely unstable, and the expatriates living there helped one another by exchanging information.

The young diplomat Peter fell in love at first sight with Celia from Trinidad-Tobago. She had dark eyes that looked as if she was hiding a deep sorrow, a charming upturned nose, and soft, warm lips. Although Peter always behaved discreetly befitted as a British diplomat, his heart was moved by a storm of passion. It was not even six months since they had first met when Peter made up his mind to share the rest of his life with Celia.

During the following five years, Peter returned to London, and Celia to the headquarters of the World Bank in Washington. Though separated by the Atlantic, they became attracted to each other all the more.

Last October Peter was appointed Governor of the British Virgin Islands, and wasted no time in inviting Celia for Christmas. With mixed feelings of apprehension and anticipation, Celia arrived at the small airport of Tortola on the one of the islands. Peter, accompanied by a uniformed aide-de-camp, met Celia at the airport. To her disappointment, Peter, who behaved in public with reserve, didn't open his arms to embrace her like a Frenchman, but only smiled and held out his hand.

In a black Jaguar they headed for Government House. The sun was shining brilliantly in a land of everlasting summer, while in Washington, D.C., people were shivering in their overcoats. Government House stood on the hilltop, and the balcony had a view of the ocean dotted with yachts. A photograph of a young and beautiful Queen Elizabeth hung on the wall of the living room, which was furnished with English style furniture. A white-aproned maid brought in tea. "You must be tired," said Peter. Celia, after having a sip of tea, said, "I am all right." She was more concerned about Peter's haggard look. She wondered if he was leading a stressful life as Governor of the colony, no matter how small it was.

Night fell. Peter and Celia went out onto the balcony to find the full moon and a myriad of stars. The air started to feel chilly. Peter, who was sitting in the chair next to Celia's, stood up and went into the room. When he came back with a blanket, Celia stood up too. "You must be cold"—so saying, Peter put the blanket over Celia's shoulders, and pulled her closer to him. It was a long kiss. Peter's strong, tall body supported Celia, who could no longer keep standing.

"Will you marry me?"

"Yes," replied Celia in a firm though low voice.

A busy life was awaiting Celia in Washington in the New Year. Although people told her that she had not gained weight, the skirts she used to wear in Uganda no longer fit her. She started dieting under the guidance of a diet consultant, and also worked out in the exercise room in the basement of the World Bank. She deliberately ordered a wedding dress that was much too small for her. It would be a disaster if she could not wear it at the wedding scheduled four months later.

On Saturday, April 25, 1992, in the garden of Government House in the British Virgin Islands, some eighty people from 23 different countries were waiting for the bride to arrive. The groom was also waiting, clad in full dress uniform and wearing a sabre. Red and yellow flowers of hibiscus and poinsettia were blooming in profusion, and the sky over the land of everlasting summer was clear and blue as always.

The doors of the Jaguar opened. Celia stepped out, helped by an escort. Having lost weight, Celia looked like a fashion model. Her wedding dress was an elegant pink, and she smiled contentedly with an assured air. "Beautiful!" someone whispered, deeply moved.

The Church of England bishop, clad in red vestments, with his hand on a black Bible, preached, "Marriage is perseverance. Today's excitement may fade in time. But you must persevere . . ." The 'Ave Maria' was sung by Katrine, a blonde Scottish woman. Her pleasant soprano voice soared to the blue sky. In the shade of a palm tree, away from the other guests, I was looking at the bride. I said to her in my mind, "You look beautiful today." Celia, who was my secretary, is not coming back to me.

The Singlehood Syndrome

"If you marry me: 1) I will fix breakfast for you every day, 2) I will make love to you even when you are eighty, and 3) I will make you laugh every day. So please marry me." I remember reading in an essay by Michiko Miyamoto, a writer, that once a Westerner had proposed to her in this manner. Since I have never lived in any foreign country other than the U.S., for convenience sake, I replace her "Westerner" with "American." So, that is the kind *koroshimonku* (flattery) American men use to win women's hearts. Iwanami's *Kojien* (Japanese dictionary) gives the definition of the word *koroshimonku* as "phrases used between men and women to win each other's hearts, or words used in general to charm people." I wonder if these phrases make American women succumb.

Breakfast—one of the utmost luxuries Americans dream of is to have breakfast in bed, brought in on a tray by a servant, and to sip hot aromatic coffee, leaning back in the bed. "I will fix breakfast for you" means "I will treat you like a queen." That should not make anyone feel unpleasant.

Make love—it seems rather unrealistic for most women of 80 years of age and their husbands, who are most likely to be older, to make love to each other. Quite a few men become impotent after 40, and this has become a social problem. A man may occasionally experience the misery of sexual inability when he makes love to the same woman for years and years. It is not that he does not love the woman. It is just his body does not function the way he wishes. I do not know if this is an aspect of the impotency which urologists discuss in medical conferences. For instance, if he had the chance to explore the soft lips of the female assistant who brings him tea when he arrives at work, and if matters between them made progress, then he might be able to perform as well as when he was young. This is not what is called impotency in medical terms. It is a very circumstantial impotency that depends on the partner. Women are aware of this, too. Nevertheless, they are moved by men's sentiment in saying that they will make love to them even when they are 80. Women think, "It doesn't matter if they actually make love or not at 80. A man who says that much will surely pay attention to me." Woman's desire to monopolize a man's attention is universal.

Make her laugh—First Lady Barbara Bush often says to the White House correspondents, "George is wonderful. He always makes me laugh." What can you do to make women laugh? Should you get a book of jokes, stuff your head with them, and repeat them on appropriate occasions? Not necessarily. What you should do is to put a woman in a happy frame of mind, so that she may smile at small things. In order to do this, you have to conduct yourself well and give top priority to your home. No matter how witty the joke you tell a woman, she will not laugh if she has just found out about your love affair. But even if your joke is very conventional, she will laugh if she is contented. If you consider the matter carefully, it is not an easy thing to make women laugh.

Now the U.S. is experiencing a singlehood syndrome—there are a great many single men and women in their 20s, 30s, and 40s in Washington. Someone told me that four out of five women in Washington are single. Most of them are highly educated and in the upper income brackets. I wonder what the reasons are. It is said that they do not want to tie themselves down by making such a serious commitment as marriage. It is not just men who make a commitment. Women do, too. Another probable and practical reason is that it is no longer inconvenient to stay unmarried. In Washington, "single men's households do not get infested with maggots." You can have a cleaner come in once a week and your apartment will be kept immaculate, and she can also do your laundry. This leaves the possibility of mental instability and the problem of sex, but I suppose these are solvable problems.

I find this syndrome quite depressing, for I belong to an older generation which believes that the prosperity of society is possible only when men and women marry and have families.

To Stop Being Human

The weather was fine on Sunday, January 13, 1991, two days before the U.S. declared it would attack Iraq if Iraqi troops did not withdraw from Kuwait by then. I asked the taxi driver to take me to the National Gallery and he asked me, "Old or New?" I answered "New" at random. I thought the fine pictures in the museum would cheer my spirits. The taxi went past the back of the White House. It was quiet there with no demonstrators. Until the previous day, there had been fiery demonstrations daily, with men and women marching and carrying placards saying "No blood for oil."

On January 12, three days before the deadline, the U.S. Congress had approved President Bush's proposal to attack Iraq. On August 2, 1990, as soon as the news that Iraq had invaded Kuwait reached Washington, the U.S. had dispatched 100,000 soldiers to Saudi Arabia, as if to say that the best way to put a quick stop to Saddam Hussein's irrational act was to confront him with force, rather than to try to solve the problem by negotiating. A majority of the American population supported President Bush. Fighter planes took off from various bases in the U.S., tanks were loaded onto cargo vessels at ports, and huge aircraft carriers and battleships departed for the Persian Gulf. The U.S. threatened Saddam Hussein, shaking its fist, "Intruder, leave Kuwait, otherwise we will teach you a lesson."

More and more troops were sent to Saudi Arabia, and when the number of soldiers reached 400,000, the most to be dispatched since World War II, the American people began to wonder why they had to go this far. The Republicans were soundly defeated by the Democrats in the election of November

1990, one of the reasons for the defeat being the deployment of troops in Saudi Arabia.

The *Washington Post* conducted a public opinion poll, the results of which were as follows:

"If Iraqi troops did not withdraw from Kuwait by the deadline of January 15, do you think the U.S. should force them out by going to war?"

Yes—63% No—32%

"Should the U.S. do so, even if 1,000 soldiers are to be killed in the war?"

Yes—44% No—53%

"Should the U.S. do so, even if 10,000 soldiers are to be killed?"

Yes—35% No—61%

Although they have a strong indignation against Iraq for unlawfully occupying Kuwait, and they feel that confrontation is necessary in order to oust the intruder, they feel reluctant if it is going to cost 1,000 lives. They feel even more reluctant if it is going to cost 10,000 lives, and this is very natural.

It was dull on Wall Street at that time, due to the continuous fall of stocks. "It must be hitting your firm hard," I said to my American friend who manages a securities firm. "I am not even sure if we can survive through the year," his face clouded.

I did not feel the same sort of tension in Japan where I went to visit from the end of the year through the New Year holidays. I am sure some Japanese lost one third or even half of their assets because of the slump. I was surprised by the firm belief among economists and businessmen that the Japanese economy is still strong. I realized strongly that the U.S. and Japan were two very different countries.

For three days from January 10, Senators and Congressmen had had ardent discussions. As I watched the telecast, many of them cried, "For whose benefit are we trying to keep peace in the

Middle East? We produce in our own country half of the oil we consume. It is Japan which imports most of its oil. Moreover, 70% of its imports are from the Middle East. In a way, we are going to shed the blood of our youth for the sake of Japan." On television a commentator said that not only had Japan not sent any personnel to the Middle East, they had only contributed a quarter of the two billion dollars they had promised. During commercial breaks, Japanese cars were advertised. What the commentator said may not have been correct. But Japan had become a target for criticism. The U.S. is so dissatisfied with Japan that no matter what Japan says it will only be taken for excuses.

Ironically, it is Japanese innovation in computers and communication technology that has made dramatic progress. But the human brain, which created the supercomputer, also invented the fearful destructive power called "nuclear weapons." Not only did it invent nuclear weapons, it used them on Hiroshima and Nagasaki, taking tens of thousands of lives away in an instant, and causing aftereffects for the survivors and their descendants for no one knows how long.

Human beings consume things extravagantly, destroying nature and increasingly polluting the earth in the process. Human being are sinful animals. Are we still going to kill one another using chemical weapons and so forth? Lately I have developed a real distrust of human beings. I feel disgusted to be a human myself. I feel like I should stop being human.

The National Gallery of Art in Washington is one of the most outstanding museums in the world. When I entered the new wing, I saw that an exhibition of photographs by Paul Strand was going on. Born in the late 19th century in New York, he left many photographic masterpieces, which are very like paintings with a literary atmosphere. Americans in jeans and sweaters were quietly appreciating the photographs.

The Bitter Taste of Spareribs

Tuesday, January 15. I felt so restless that I decided to go out. It was ten o'clock at night in midwinter, but the breeze felt lukewarm on my face. A twenty-minute walk eastward on F Street from the Watergate Hotel took me to the White House. Its facade was lit by searchlights and was clearly silhouetted, while all around was pitch dark. About five hundred demonstrators were walking in circles in front of the White house. Every one of them had a candle in his hand and they were all silent. If you demonstrate by crying out loud at night, you will be suppressed immediately by the police. Unlike in Japan, demonstrations are not systematized in the U.S. People participate individually in accordance with their own principles and beliefs. It is a different behavior pattern from that of the Japanese, who prefer group activity.

In only two hours it was going to be decided whether to go to war or not. American public opinion was divided in two. These silent demonstrators in front of the White House were against rushing into war. But at that point, President Bush, who was then on the second floor of the White House, had already made the decision that if Saddam Hussein did not withdraw his troops from Kuwait by the deadline set, the U.S. would attack Iraq. There was no time to waste. On the 16th of January, despite the prayers of the people against it, the war broke out.

Sunday, January 20. I had long meant to go to Roosevelt Island, which is situated in the Potomac River opposite the Watergate, but had never done so. Putting on my Reebok sneakers and a turtleneck sweater, I left my Watergate apartment. The sky was blue and clear, and the air was warm like a spring day. In front of the Embassy of Saudi Arabia, which is located across the street from the Watergate, security guards with long guns were keeping watch. Although it had been four days since the start of the war, and 450,000 soldiers were fighting in Saudi Arabia, I did not feel any tension in the neighborhood. After having a peep at the Kennedy Center, I crossed Roosevelt Bridge and arrived at the Island at one o'clock. It took me one hour to get there because I walked rather slowly, but walking briskly it would have taken only half an hour.

The island, with its virgin forest, in which it is a little frightening to be alone, even during the day, lies in the middle of the river. On the island stands a large bronze statue of Theodore Roosevelt. The width of the Potomac there is about 1,000 meters. The spring-like sun was shining on the surface of the water. The clock tower of Georgetown University, which looks like the Parliament Building in London, could be seen at a distance. Everything around looked so open and spacious. I pondered over the country called the United States of America. It is amazing that they made such a heroic decision to start a war, which not only may cost many lives but also will certainly cost a tremendous amount of money. Every time a missile is fired from a fighter, it costs the country a million dollars. What are they thinking of when they already have a number of serious problems such as the budget deficit, the trade deficit, savings and loan scandals, narcotic trafficking, environmental pollution, and so forth? America seems always to shoulder responsibility for the deeds of the entire world. They did so in the Vietnam War, and with the boat people. When I first came to America on the *Hikawa-maru* in 1956, I was impressed with everything I saw for its vastness. How on earth could Japan ever fight against a country of such enormous scale? I simply could not understand it. Where has that gigantic America gone? The country still looks wealthy and beautiful as far as I can see. Foreigners who have experienced life in America never seem to want to go back to their own country. I know a Japanese pediatrician who has been in America for 32 years. Where he lives in Virginia is only about 30 minutes by car from Washington, D.C. "I have never been back to Japan in 32 years," he says as if it is nothing unusual. America's generous and open attitude toward foreigners, and, more than anything else, its comfortable domestic environment, which is attainable as long as you work hard—these are probably the factors that make foreigners want to live permanently in America. The more I think about America, the more difficult I find it to understand the country.

The CNN broadcasts news 24 hours a day. They have correspondents not only in the White House and the Pentagon, but also at the front lines in Iraq and Saudi Arabia, so you can watch the war in your own living room as if you are actually there. I could not help being glued to the television even before the deadline of January 15. This kind of war was unprecedented. The correspondent who remained in Baghdad until the deadline to report from there was received as a hero when he finally came back to America. "There was hardly anything left to eat. I survived for three days eating tins of salmon and candy bars I had bought in Washington," said the unshaven reporter, who usually appeared lightly made up on television. "This is the CNN War, rather than the Gulf War," a Japanese journalist stationed in Washington murmured, smiling wryly. On January 20th, during television coverage of the Hawaiian Open Golf Tournament, each player sent a message between plays: "Our fellow-countrymen fighting in the Gulf, please come back soon." I too wish from the bottom of my heart, "Come back soon."

I crossed Key Bridge from Roosevelt Island and strolled in Georgetown. Georgetown, which has many sophisticated boutiques and fancy restaurants, is in the District of Columbia and is the district of the young people, like Harajuku or Roppongi in Tokyo. I saw long-legged young men, in jeans deliberately ripped open at the knees, biting into spareribs as if they had nothing to worry about.

Men's Tears

The face of a soldier, a dark man of about 50, came up on the television screen in close-up. He looked like a typical sergeant who had worked his way up from a lowly rank. No sooner had I noticed the tears in his eyes, than they started to run in large drops down his cheeks. The man was watching the "Superbowl" on television from a military base in Saudi Arabia.

American football is by far the most popular sport, more than baseball, basketball, or golf. The Superbowl, which decides the final victor among the professional teams, is much more dominant than the deciding sumo match between Futabayama and Akinoumi, the Waseda-Keio baseball game (up to about 1955), the Giant-Tigers baseball game (up to about 1975), and the final round of high-school baseball in Koshien, all combined together. The show before the play-off is gayer than "*Kohaku-utagassen*"* ever was, even in its heyday. It is one grand national event. President Bush watched it on television with his wife, Barbara, and he gave a televised address to the whole nation, which was glued to the ABC Network on the evening of January 27th when the Superbowl was aired. The stadium in Tampa, Florida, was filled with 75,000 spectators. Whitney Houston sang the American national anthem.

Perhaps a thousand emotions crowded the sergeant's mind listening to the national anthem. The sergeant and the young soldiers eagerly watching the football game appeared on television intermittently. It was 2:00 AM in Saudi Arabia.

The ground war in Kuwait is about to begin. When it does, they will have to go to the fromt. My heart goes out to the innocent-looking soldiers enjoying watching the football game. Sometimes when the young soldiers are interviewed for televi-

---

**Kohaku-utagassen:* a famous national singing competition broadcast every New Year's Eve sion, their faces begin to twist as if they are about to cry. When that happens the image on the screen changes immediately. They are my son's age, and so I cannot be indifferent. It must be a terrifying thing to fight in a war. Men's tears often strike me with awe. It is perhaps because men's tears are never shed by acting.

On the day following the outbreak of the war, a Japanese woman in kimono visited the Pentagon. It was Kiharu Nakamura who resides in New York. Miss Nakamura was a geisha in Shimbashi as described in her book *The Story of an Edokko Geisha*. She has been living in New York since 1956 and she teaches Kouta and Nagauta to Americans and Japanese, while working as an operatic consultant. "The U.S. soldiers deployed in Saudi Arabia are on duty in a very harsh environment far away from home, while we enjoy Christmas and New Year's Day with out families. Our hearts go out to them and their families back home, and to express our feelings, here is our contribution, though it is small." Miss Nakamura took the initiative of collecting donations from Japanese living in New York, Washington, and Los Angeles. About $4,000 was collected. The Japanese people living in the U.S. have very mixed feelings toward the Gulf War. President Bush very quickly deployed the U.S. troops in the Gulf and prepared for an all-out attack, and the U.N. set the deadline for January 15 in support of Bush's decision. The whole world kept hoping until the last minute that the Iraqi troops would withdraw from Kuwait and so avoid going to war. But the situation has come to a climax. Many Japanese may criticize the U.S. for its militaristic policy, snap judgment, and sense of supremacy. Only history will tell us later how to punish an outlaw who disturbs the world order. But it is a fact that 400,000 American soldiers are in Saudi Arabia, and that makes Japanese living in America feel guilty and uncomfortable. The television reports almost every day that Japan depends on oil from the Middle East more than any other country, and that the U.S. is protecting Japan at the risk of American lives. Living in the U.S., you can feel the war acutely, unlike in Japan.

Kiharu Nakamura came to Washington all the way from New York to give the contribution money, and letters from children, to Carl Ford, Deputy Assistant Secretary for East Asian and Pacific Affairs. A young Japanese diplomat who had accompanied her was touched by the act, and had to dash to the rest room to hide his tears. "It took me by surprise. I don't remember when I last cried," he told me bashfully later. I can only imagine what his tears signify. He who, as a diplomat, keeps in close contact with the U.S. government, must have been disgusted by the indecisive attitude of the Japanese government, which is always late in making decisions. I suppose this pure-hearted diplomat could not help weeping, moved to find that there was someone like Miss Nakamura among the Japanese people, and also frustrated by the Japanese government's insensibility in not understanding the goodwill of Japanese citizens like Miss Nakamura.

Men cry when they are moved or frightened rather than when they are sad. Come to think of it, it has been ages since I last did so. Surprisingly, I did not cry when my mother passed away. I kissed her on the forehead when they put her body into the coffin. She felt cold to my lips. But I did not cry. Some men hammered nails into the coffin with rocks, and opened a small window of the coffin for me, saying that it would be the last time I would see her. I saw her white face. Presently I felt something coming rapidly from the back of my nose, and it reached my eyes in no time. But I could not indulge in tears because I was the chief mourner and had to manage the whole business of the funeral. I had to control myself.

I wonder if it is because men cry only when they can no longer suppress the tears that I am always struck by men's tears. The tears and the distorted faces of the soldiers in Saudi Arabia are perhaps nothing but their expression of their fear that they may die at any minute. Perhaps, like urinating when frightened, tears automatically gush from their eyes. But such reasoning by me is not a matter of consequence. I wish for a prompt cease-fire and the safe and quick return of the troops.

Attaboy, George!

Lately I have been watching CNN television day in and day out. Normally I turn the television off when I do other things, but ever since the Gulf War began I feel so apprehensive that I keep the television on all the time.

On February 27, at nine o'clock sharp, President Bush suddenly appeared on the television screen. "Kuwait has been liberated. Iraq has surrendered." Without any introduction, he started the speech. He did not have that tormented look on his face, but looked relieved, as if he was about to start laughing. His speech did not last more than ten minutes.

I was watching television lying on the bed, but I jumped up because I somehow felt I could not stay there. I dashed to the bathroom and washed my face with cold water. Looking at my wet face in the mirror I murmured to myself, "I am so glad."

The CNN had General Schwarzkopf on. The explanation of strategies by Schwarzkopf, who is said to have an IQ of 170, was clear and succinct. And yet it was not done in a cold bureaucratic manner. He had the air of the man next door with whom you feel at ease. The titles of the CNN programs changed progressively: "Gulf Crisis" until the war began on January 16, "Gulf War" as soon as the war started, "Gulf Talk" after Bush's announcement of a cease-fire, then "Toward Peace in the Gulf."

The next morning I was with a middle-aged American man in the elevator of the Watergate. "I am glad the war is over," I said to him. He said "So am I, but there are heaps of domestic issues to be solved. It won't be easy for President Bush," and smiled.

I went directly to my nine o'clock dental appointment. Dr. Kaihara, a fourth generation Japanese-American, spoke to me after giving me a shot of anesthetic, "The war is really over, isn't it? Saddam Hussein has really accepted our demands, hasn't he?" "Yes, the war is certainly over," I said, forcing open my lips which were beginning to feel numb.

It is only about 15-minute walk from the dentist's office to my office, but I picked up a taxi, for I somehow felt impatient. I said to the taxi driver, "To the World Bank," and the driver said in English with a heavy accent, "OK, but I wish the bank would disappear soon." "Why do you say such a thing? The Bank makes loans to the poor countries." "It's the dictators of the poor countries the World Bank actually makes loans to," he said recklessly. I had never heard anyone criticize the World Bank so boldly, so I asked him just before I got out of the taxi, "Where are you from?" and he said "I am from Zambia."

I walked to the White House after lunch. The air in the morning was cold enough to need a scarf around the neck, but it was much warmer in the afternoon. Quite a few people were already carrying their overcoats in their hands.

A man was demonstrating right in front of the White House, carrying a placard with "ATTABOY, GEORGE!" written in large letters. I took a close look at the man and found that he wore a mask of George Bush.

If the survey of popular support of the President was conducted now, I suppose Bush would get an unprecedented percentage of support. President Bush risked his political life on the Gulf War. He received severe criticism from Americans, as well as from those of other countries, for his immovable determination in deploying 500,000 soldiers. But he never departed from his beliefs, using his now famous "Bushphone" to explain the situation moment by moment to President Gorbachev, Prime Minister Major, President Mitterrand, and Prime Minister Kaifu. This hit the nail right on the head. The whole nation is excited over the successful operation forcing the Iraqi troops out of Kuwait with minimal damage.

Ghassan El-Rifai, Vice President of MIGA, came into my office. "I hear Japan is contributing another nine billion dollars to the Gulf. They initially contributed four billion, and then nine billion, and if they are contributing another nine billion, it will add up to the enormous sum of 22 billion dollars." "No, no, you are mistaken," I tried to correct his misunderstanding. It has been a long time since the number nine billion appeared in the newspapers. Maybe some Americans think that the first nine billion has been given already, and the second is being approved in the Diet now.

"It was an unseasonably warm day in early March. Several kids in my class began bullying me during the break. They had the habit of chasing after me, saying, 'Japan is unfair,' but it was worse that day. They grew violent while I tried to stay composed and unconcerned, and they kicked and pushed me. When I fell on the ground, they threw rocks at me. One of the rocks hit me in the eye and it hurt. I ran to the pipe that was lying in the corner of the schoolyard and took refuge, and then I cried . . . When I returned home I told my mother what had happened at school. She looked increasingly sad, and lowered her eyes. She was sobbing. I said cheerfully, 'I am thinking of giving a lecture to the class on Chinese characters,' and smiled at her. Tears kept falling down her cheeks. I wiped her tears with a tissue and she finally said, "We will never give up, shall we?"

This is part of a composition by Tomohiko Washimi, a third grader, written for his Washington Japanese School class. He concludes his composition with: "They always abuse me saying 'Japan is unfair,' but I am not dejected. Believing in 'face up to everything,' I decided to teach Chinese characters to the bullying kids and they have finally accepted me. 'Face up to everything' is my favorite phrase."

Not only adults, but even Japanese children living in America are experiencing hardship.

Class Reunion

On a Saturday in late April, I was waiting at Kennedy Airport when four of my high school classmates and their wives trooped out of the plane. We were born in 1931 and are sixty this year. One of them had suggested that together with our wives we celebrate our 60th birthdays in America, and it was realized. They all looked fine despite the 13-hour flight from Tokyo. Our plans were to spend one week in New York and Washington, for the men to enjoy golf and the women shopping.

First of all, there is Y. We all call him "Pawnbroker." He is the only son of a pawnbroker in Sugamo and is indulgent and otherworldly. He is an accredited master of the Tadé School of Kouta, a traditional form of Japanese song. He can play golf and tennis reasonably well. Wearing a red golf hat on his bald head, he strides around not caring a bit about his paunchy belly. He works for a computer software company.

And then there is K, who answers "*Haiyo* (Yup)" when called "*Sensei.*" We do not know exactly what he does, even though we have known him for years and years. He is a "consultant." He has long black hair, a moustache, is five feet four inches tall, long-torsoed, short-legged, and sun tanned, with a healthy complexion and mischievous, beady eyes. He is different.

N is called "Secretary-General" because he is the organizer of this trip. We could call him "Secretary" without the "General," but N has an air that makes us want to call him "Secretary-General." It is because he gives himself an air of importance and loves to lecture. He has a good color sense and is well-dressed. His handsome profile could make a picture, if he sat at the counter of a bar in Ginza, quietly having a drink all by himself.

There are quite a few "Presidents" among my friends, but no one is a match for M in terms of their length of experience as a president. His family has been in the interior decorating business since his grandfather's time. It has been some ten years since M succeeded his father. Born and brought up near Korakuen, he is a true Tokyo metropolitan. He tends to jump to conclusions, often leading to mistakes, and does make blunders, but he is a very honest man. His hair, which has largely turned grey, falls over his broad forehead.

Rockefeller donated Central Park to New York City under the condition that it be solely used as a "park"; therefore, the erection of any buildings is not permitted. However, there is one restaurant. It is called "Tavern on the Green," and it is like Matsumoto-ro in Hibiya Park in Tokyo. The restaurant is surrounded by dense woods and on the branches of the trees are thousands of tiny lights. At night the illuminated trees look as if they are floating in the darkness. This type of decoration is very popular in America during the Christmas season, but you can see it here throughout the year.

On a Sunday evening, five couples went in a van to the restaurant to celebrate birthdays. Although it was seven o'clock, it was still as light as day, and the small lights on the trees did not yet have their full effect. The setting was perfect, with a coach and a top-hatted driver, and an old-fashioned tavern, except that the night was still to fall.

The entrance hall was crowded with people. Waiters in tuxedos were shouting at the patrons from a raised box which resembled the watch stand at a Japanese public bath. Twenty to thirty patrons in front of them were shouting back. They were arguing about whether they had reservations or not. It was a warning to us. We had made a reservation, but they told us brusquely that they did not have it. There was no point in arguing with the waiters. We decided that there was no alternative for us but to wait, so we went out to the garden. The husbands have aged in their own way but the wives are still quite attractive. Especially tonight, they look lively dressed in their best clothes.

"President" is looking closely at the wiring on the tree branches, presumably with a future reference to his business. "Sensei" has fallen asleep sitting on a bench. "Pawnbroker" is impatiently walking back and forth. "Secretary-General" has been earnestly admonishing the wives about how dangerous a place New York is.

Night fell by 8:30. The breeze felt pleasant on my face, and the area was filled with the smell of the trees. A table had not yet become available. I asked "Secretary-General" to collect everyone, and proposed that we give up and go to a Japanese restaurant. Everyone was getting impatient and unanimously agreed to my proposal. We got in the van and headed for Mugi on 58th Street.

We begged the proprietor, who was reluctant to have us, because it was Sunday night and he did not have much in stock, and found our way into the restaurant. There was a single customer there but he soon left, intimidated by the unusual group. "Very good. Now we can talk freely," said "*Sensei,*" whose voice is naturally loud, as he started talking. "Secretary-General" interrupted him and poured beer for everyone, then proposed a toast. We had spinach with soy sauce, beef with potatoes, chopped burdock root, fried fish cakes, salted salmon, and noodles. We were supposed to have been having French food by candlelight and talking in low voices. "Pawnbroker" sang "*Tatsumi yoitoko,*" a traditional Japanese song.

The wives were saying: "We should do this again in ten years when they are seventy."

"That's a good idea, but someone may be missing then."

The men had switched from beer to saké as the women left that poignant remark behind and poured the clear saké into their husbands' empty cups.

6

Thoughts on the Future

Final Abode

The pain of the seat belt cutting into my stomach woke me up. The pilot did not make a very smooth landing. I realized that I had slept all the way from Boston, which we had left at seven o'clock in the evening. Still feeling dazed, I murmured to myself, "Back in Washington . . ." I did not feel as if I had come home. I picked up a taxi outside the terminal of National Airport. To my right flowed the broad Potomac.

I had gone to Boston the previous morning to give a speech at the Japan-America Society and watch the Waseda-Keio football game at Harvard Stadium. Initially I had thought that a Waseda-Keio joint team was to play against the Harvard team. But, even though the Harvard team may not be top caliber, a Japanese college team would not be any competition. It turned out to be a Waseda vs. Keio match to be played at the stadium of the prestigious Harvard University.

The Keio team was intensively trained by a Harvard coach for four days, and the Waseda team by a Yale coach. During the match, the American coaches were more spirited than the Japanese players. It looked as if Waseda was going to win, but 38 seconds before the game finished, Keio had a touchdown and Waseda was defeated by the narrow margin of 19 to 21.

The taxi driver, irritated by the slow driver of the car in front of him, blew his horn. The car was being driven by an old lady. I had not had a wild taxi driver for a long time, I thought. The taxi crossed the Memorial Bridge and drove into Washington, D.C. Lincoln Memorial and the Kennedy Center came into view.

It has been three years since I came to Washington, D.C., which is as beautiful as a park. I do not know how much longer I will live here. I have mixed feelings; on the one hand, I have had enough of Washington, and yet I would also like to stay here a little longer.

You will be disillusioned if you come to Washington expecting it to be as big a city as New York or Chicago. When America declared Independence in 1776, Philadelphia was the capital, but Washington became the capital in 1800. The population of Washington at that time was only 3,200. Now the population during the day is one million. The town was planned from the beginning as the capital of the nation by the French planner L'Enfant, hence it bears a similarity to Paris and Versailles. The man-made capital is surrounded by beautiful "country." Only half an hour's drive from the White House will bring you to residential areas, more densely wooded than Hakone or Karuizawa.

Washington may be thought of as a man-made city surrounded by southern villages, rather than as a big city. People live in single houses in the suburbs leading a simple and sound life. In the morning they put on a tie and drive half an hour to work. In the evening, they drive home, kiss their wives, change into shorts, tend the lawn since the day is still young, and then enjoy a barbecue in the garden with their families.

After six o'clock in the evening, the center of Washington, where MIGA is located, becomes dead, with very few pedestrians. Only out-of-towners visiting Washington on business for a few days will be walking on the streets of the area at night. There is a busier area called Dupont Circle, which is similar in atmosphere to New York's Greenwich Village. But it is much smaller in scale and not nearly as sophisticated.

About one hundred Japanese companies and banks have offices in Washington. Since the purpose of these offices is not business, but to gather information, the Japanese representatives are more of the researcher type. They are modest and intelligent, they do everything properly, and without exception they all live in elegant single houses with beautiful wives.

Among the Japanese representatives living in New York, there are quite a few who are there alone while their families are back in Japan. They feel compelled to lead knavish lives, going to karaoke bars night after night and playing mahjong until dawn, whereas the representatives residing in Washington lead most refined and imperturbable lives.

Most of the parties in Washington hosted by the Japanese companies and banks include spouses. The husbands leave work at six, go home, take a shower, change, put on some cologne, and drive to the party with their wives, both of them dressed to the nines. They can easily arrive by seven. The parties are lively because there are equal numbers of men and women. They talk and talk and eat everything from French-style hors d'oeuvre, sushi, and yakitori, and roast beef to chocolate mousse and espresso until they go home. They are never so impolite as to leave one party after only 30 minutes to go to another, like New York representatives do. Washington's parties have poise and style.

For many years I had led a nervous life, constantly feeling pressed for time, looking at my watch and thinking about my schedule. Everything I saw and heard in Washington was new to me. I had expected to see those big city's characteristics such as filth, nihilism, guiltiness, an extreme disparity in wealth, and evil influences hovering about—which shows how ignorant I was. I am finally beginning to adjust after living here for three years. The pace of life in Washington may be more suitable for someone my age. Sometimes I think about making Washington my final abode.

Thoughts on the Toilet

I looked for the flush lever on the toilet at Dulles Airport, but I couldn't find it. It is usually within reach of your right hand in a seated position, or else it is located to your left. Sometimes you need to stand up and press a pedal. I looked around desperately but still I could not find it. I thought I might have missed it because I have been getting senile, so I looked in every nook and cranny again with the utmost care, concentrating all my attention. I stood there, feeling helpless, when the water spurted out and flushed everything down. The toilet had an automatic flush system. I pushed the door open, feeling exhausted from looking so hard for the flushing mechanism, and bothered by the irritation and sense of helplessness I had felt when unable to find it. I tried to think calmly as I washed my hands. What's the point of having an automatic flush system? I wonder if it's because some people forget to flush. If there is a constant demand, such as in the rest rooms at Narita Airport (I do not know if it's just my experience, but whenever I am there all the toilets are always occupied and I have never been able to use them without waiting), whoever uses the toilet after an imprudent person who forgot to flush will have to take care of it. I often find the rest rooms at Dulles Airport completely empty with not a single person in them. It is possible that if someone forgets to flush, a toilet may remain unflushed for an hour or two, or even overnight. If that is the case it is very insanitary. I wonder if this is the reason for the automatic flush.

The toilets on the new planes All Nippon Airways flies between Washington and Tokyo are quite confusing if you are not familiar with them. Water does not come out when you flush. Instead, with a stange "zap" noise everything disappears. And you stare at the toilet wondering if you have operated it properly. I do not understand the way it works. Probably it is by vacuum suction, but because it is too delicate a subjcct to ask young stewardesses, I have yet to find out how it works.

I attended a cocktail party last night at a hotel in Washington. People were talking in groups of four and five, each person holding a glass in their hand. Irene, a journalist, began to tell of her recent experience in Paris. She is a beautiful woman in her early 30s, and a very good conversationalist. She told us she went to a toilet in a museum in Paris. It was pitch dark. She felt the walls for a light switch to no avail. When she stepped inside, the light came on, and when she put her hands under the faucet, water came out. Then as she left the toilet, feeling slightly disoriented, the light went off. "I felt so uneasy," she said, and everyone nodded in sympathy. Some people were simply agreeing to the subject of the story, but I suppose others were surprised, or even moved, to hear a factual story from an elegant woman about her going to a toilet, even though it is a natural act.

I remember being surprised when I sat on a "Washlet" at a friend's home in Japan. Everything is automatically taken care of by pressing numerous buttons on the right—comfortably warm water will wash you, and warm air will dry you. It was also equipped with a bidet. The "Washlet" is an invention of which Japan can be proud. It was completed after many experiments with the equipment, studying subtle differences of angle for both the "bottom washer" and the bidet. That is typically Japanese. And "Washlet" is such a delightful Japanese-English word. I sometimes see television commercials for hemorrhoid remedies, so I suppose many Americans suffer from this problem. And I suppose many American women wish to use a bidet, though recently-built houses and apartments are not equipped with one. "Washlets" will perhaps sell dramatically in America. Or maybe the producers have already found a market in the U.S.

Kappa Senoo, the author of *Kappa Peeped,* once serialized in a magazine some very detailed illustrations of celebrities' toilets as seen from above. I suppose Senoo undertook this when an editor of the magazine sought out unusual toilets, flattered the owners that their admirers would appreciate seeing the toilets, and persuaded those who were a little reluctant to publicize their toilets. It is not particularly strange to make an elaborate toilet, because after all it is where one spends a total of at least one hour every day.

My bathroom is significantly larger than that in an average Japanese apartment. It has a fairly large bathtub, large enough for me with a height of 1.74 meters (5 feet 8 inches), to lie in with only my feet sticking out, as well as a toilet and a bidet. The building is 30 years old. Perhaps it used to have more European tenants or people who had spent some time in Europe, for whom a bidet was a necessity. The bathroom is nothing special and will not stir Kappa Senoo's desire to illustrate. On top of the toilet I keep chronologies of Japanese and world history in editions used for preparing for university entrance examinations, a Sanseido English-Japanese dictionary, and a pair of reading glasses.

In the morning, sitting on the toilet, I read the *Washington Post.* I do not bother to consult a dictionary even if I encounter words I do not know the meaning of, because I find it too tiresome, unless I am completely at a loss. I sometimes read the chronological tables. Since I am so ignorant of history as a result of disliking my high-school history teacher, I read them avidly, for everything is new to me, even things that may be common knowledge for most people.

Aspirations

I have been thinking lately about the ultimate goal of life and the right way to live. It is, so to speak, the question of what to live for. I do not think I have changed very much. I think much the same now at the age of sixty as when I was a young man of twenty. I do not know if I was mature for twenty, or if I have grown older without maturing. Perhaps the latter is the case. I wonder where I got my ambitious, realistic way of looking at life, why I had my mind set on money so much. I wonder if it was because I was poor.

I do not want to criticize the young, which is typically done by starting with some such phrase as "today's young are . . .," even though I have entered the category of the old. The youngsters of today appear to me to shine, while I, at their age, was decadent but calculating.

I spent four years of junior high school in a town north of Tokyo called Sano. I had a very interesting circle of friends. Ishibashi, who had returned from Manchuria, was a great admirer of Enoken (a popular Japanese comedian) and wanted to become a comedian himself. He had large eyes, just like Enoken, and somehow did not look very Japanese. He was active in the school drama club and was a very talented actor. Sudo, who I had known since primary school, dreamt of becoming a film director. Though he was only a junior high-school student, his essay titled "A Study on the Actual Sound" was published in the magazine called "Cinema Shumpo." Kuramochi, who was also a local, had a dream of becoming a guitarist. He was able to play classical pieces that required a highly advanced technique.

They all had aspirations. I do not know what went wrong, but not one of them accomplished his original intention. I do not think it was because they were untalented, but rather because they did not have an unfaltering adherence to their dreams. They lacked tenacity. Also, they were afraid of poverty. That is why they were so cowardly. They always had a mundane adult attitude that it is essential to be able to make a decent living before pursuing youthful aspirations.

When I was about twenty, I concluded that the "right way of life" and a "happy life" were not necessarily the same. For instance, you become a doctor. You immerse yourself in a remote village and dedicate your time and energy to examining and treating villagers, turning your back on making a fortune as a practicing physician. The life of an impoverished artist who devotes himself to expressing beauty sounds noble too. I thought those were examples of the right way of life, which overlapped with poverty in my view, and I felt terrified to imagine being even more impoverished than I already was.

I chose to study economics, even though what I really wanted to study was literature, because I thought I would then have better job opportunities. I thought I would be happier if I led a peaceful and comfortable life, like being soaked in tepid water, married with children. My only excuse is that I know now that a "happy life" is not necessarily a righteous life, for it is a deceptive idea that these two are synonymous. I will always reproach myself for having been a coward who could not lead a righteous life, but instead continued living a happy life.

It is too late to have regrets, though, for I am not very far from the end of my life. But if I could start all over again I would:

1) Study what really interests me. I would not care whether it would lead to a good job or not, so long as I could make a living. It is not a big deal to work for a major company after gaining a degree in a field that you chose against your will, simply because it would lead you to a good job. The best you can expect is to feel satisfaction when you present your name card with your title and company name printed on it.
2) Not marry unless I met someone I desperately loved and could not stay away from even for a moment, and not marry for such reasons as fear of not being accepted socially if I stayed unmarried, or to avoid loneliness in my old age and seek the pleasures of a happy home.
3) Live in a circle of people with whom I can commune intimately, in harmony with nature, rather than seeking the utility and convenience of an easy life.

7

Travels in Other Lands

The Caux Round Table Conference by Lake Geneva

It was a fine day in late July. The scenery was perfect with the calm water of Lake Geneva, gigantic columns of clouds floating in a blue sky, cattle gathered in the fields, and red and yellow flowers everywhere.

My wife, our 23-year-old daughter Haruko, and I were on our way from Geneva to a village called Caux. "Switzerland is more picturesque in real life than in the postcards, isn't it?" said Mr. Fujita of MRA, who was our driver.

"World peace will not be attained if the countries vie with one another in expanding armaments. What's important is the moral and spiritual 'rearmament' of human beings"—with this claim by Dr. Frank Buckman of the U.S., the MRA (Moral Re-Armament) movement started in 1938, and Caux is the location of its world conference.

One hour's drive on a steep and winding road, which resembled Nikko's Irohazaka, took us to a house on the top of the mountain at an altitude of 1,000 meters. The mountain house, after which the castle in Walt Disney's *Cinderella* was modeled, is a large wooden structure.

No-one working there is paid. The place is run by volunteers. All those who work there—the people who open the door and take your baggage to your room upon your arrival, the people working in the kitchen, the doctors in the medical room—are volunteers. I felt good, as if I had come to a friend's place, for I was fed up with the professional social smile of the hotel bellboys and with having to figure out how much to tip. I liked the room to which we were shown. Although simple, it had two small beds. The bathtub was also to my liking. It was large and deep, and made with real ceramic, not plastic. From the windows, I could see the water of the lake, shining in the brilliant summer sun, and the sharp peaks of the Swiss Alps, which seemed so near that I felt I could almost touch them. The temperature was neither too warm nor too cold, but just right. There was always a gentle breeze.

Six hundred people, men and women, young and old, were gathered there from all over the world to attend various conferences. My wife, who was on crutches with a broken left ankle as the result of a fall on a New York street a month earlier, peeped into the kitchen to find men and women, young and middle-aged, working busily. Without a moment's hesitation she volunteered to peel the potatoes. She found a kindred spirit in a young Russian woman named Natasha, and invited her to Tokyo.

A German named Frederic who happened to sit next to me at the dinner table asked, "Can you guess how old I am?" Americans, even men, hardly ever talk about age. I wondered if it was different in Germany. I said to him, "Forty-five," and he said triumphantly with a big smile, "Sixty." He boasted that he looked young as a result of swimming every morning. A middle-aged man who happened to be there took it very seriously and challenged, "If that's the case, why don't we swim in the lake starting tomorrow." The three of us, Ronald (an American), Frederic, and I agreed to gather in the lobby at six-thirty.

At six o'clock the next morning I opened the windows to feel chilly mountain air. Thinking that it was too cold to swim, I stared at the large deep bathtub. To be honest, I would have much preferred to soak in the hot bath. I gave a deep sigh regretting the promise I had so rashly made last night. "You must go. You promised them," murmured my wife who I had thought was still asleep.

The three of us went in a car driven by Frederic down the mountain to the lake. I sank myself hesitantly into water whose surface looked like a mirror, and which was clean enough to be drinking water. It was cold. Nevertheless it was invigorating. "It is twenty-two degrees," Frederic cried. I wondered how he knew. I thought it was typically German to describe it by its temperature rather than with adjectives such as "cold" or "warm." We swam to the middle of the lake, and on until we came to Chateau de Chillon, about which Lord Byron wrote in his poem.

No alcohol is served in the mountain house. A wine-colored liquid in a wine bottle is poured into wine glasses, but it is non-alcoholic. Seven years ago I stopped drinking. Far from missing it, I have grown to dislike alcohol. Not only that, although I was a drinker myself, I now look down on drinkers. The more they drink, the more self-important they become, and the higher their voices. Their faces turn either red or white. They shout as they please, and begin to think that the world revolves around them. Poor souls. Of course I lost my drinking friends. Some of the nice people I did not want to lose left me. Sometimes I feel disgusted with myself that I have become a beastly bore. But no matter what they say I now appreciate meals without alcohol.

Late at night Natasha comes with her husband to visit us in our room. My wife says he looks just like Napoleon. "Napoleon" is a philosophy professor at the University of Moscow. Since he does not speak English, Natasha acts as an interpreter. I have never in my life spoken so intimately with Russians. They are not at all different from us, but warm, ordinary people. Politics is a monstrous thing. For many years, politics made me think that devils lived behind the iron curtain.

About the same time, Haruko was talking to a Dutch girl named Annette, lying on the grass, looking up at the starry sky.

Everyone is welcomed at the mountain house in Caux. I particularly hope the Japanese young people on whose shoulders rests the twenty-first century will visit there. It is a wonderful opportunity for them to meet young people from all over the world.

On Prince Edward Island

Lucy Maud Montgomery, the author of *Anne of Green Gables,* married Mr. McDonald, who was a minister. The female doctor I went to see on Prince Edward Island was also a McDonald, so I asked her if she was a relation. She answered with a smile, saying that when she was a little girl she asked her father if they were related, wishing that they were, but unfortunately they were not. Many people living on the island are of Scottish descent, and McDonald is a very common Scottish name.

Prince Edward Island, located in the Maritime Provinces of Canada, is about one third the size of Shikoku.* We had arrived the previous day and already I had to see a doctor. The first thing I had done on arriving at the cottage was to dash to a swimming pool which had a slide for children. I went down the slide and fell into the pool awkwardly. Instantly I felt a sharp pain in the ear. It was so severe I decided to go to see a doctor. The blonde—not red-haired—doctor, who had on a T-shirt and shorts, a far from doctor-like outfit, was a beautiful woman in her early 30s. She took a look at my ear and said that it was swollen. She prescribed penicillin. The fee was 20 Canadian dollars (at that time ¥3,000). My wife and children were sitting anxiously in the waiting room. "The doctor says it is not serious," I reported. My eldest said "I

*Shikoku: smallest of the four main Japanese islands

thought so. Dad always exaggerates things. We shall ignore him even if he says he has cancer, won't we?" And everyone nodded. The six of us headed, in two rented cars, for the house that was the setting of *Anne of Green Gables.*

My family is scattered between Washington, D.C., New York, and Tokyo, but we make it a rule to travel together at least once a year for one week. We went to Bermuda in 1989, and that was when my wife suggested Prince Edward Island for 1990. She must have been longing to visit the island ever since she read *Anne of Green Gables.* The book appeals to people, especially young girls, all over the world.

The tiny green island comes into view after a 30-minute flight from Halifax in Nova Scotia. There are sunlit golden hills, black forests of fir trees, small white houses here and there, and cattle and horses grazing in the pasture. For a while I was possessed by the illusion that I had landed in a fairyland. There were not many tourists because it was already late August and nearly the end of the peak holiday season.

I was looking at the horizon, lying on the sandy beach on a Sunday afternoon. White sea gulls were flying low over the blue sea. The beach was deserted and all I could hear was the sound of waves. Mild sun and a pleasant breeze made me feel drowsy. My children have grown. "Do you want us to make you a grandfather soon?" my daughters tease me.

In 1980, about this time of the year, the six of us had left Tokyo for New York. It was the second time for my children. Five years earlier my wife and I had returned to Tokyo with our four young children. No sooner had they adjusted to the Japanese life and language than they had to switch back to English. I did not know what was going to happen, but I was able to place all of them in a private school in Manhattan. We had no idea that our eldest daughter, Akiko, went to Central Park Zoo every morning instead of to school. We were astounded when our neighbor told us what Akiko had been doing. We rushed to the zoo to find her cleaning up the droppings in the goat pen. The school she wanted to go to was one of the most prestigious schools. We did not think she would make it but she was accepted without any difficulty thanks to a recommendation by the superintendent of the zoo. I thought it was very American.

We relocated our second oldest daughter, Haruko, in a boarding school which would very much impress Tetsuko Kuroyanagi.* All the children there, 136 junior and senior high-school girls in total, were very much like Totto-chan.* Horseback riding in the morning, drawing in the afternoon, canoeing in the evening, and having dinner with teachers—the children grew up carefree.

Our third girl, Kuniko, hated her Catholic school and decided all by herself to go back to Tokyo to live with her grandmother. And my youngest child, Seido, who was placed in third grade, also had hardships, although he never told us at the time. He now confesses that he did not understand a word of English then. People say absurdly that children learn foreign languages in no time, and that they will start quarrelling in English in two or three months. Foreign languages are not easy to learn. Even children will take a year or two to be able to speak English.

There are about 4,500 school-age Japanese children living in New York. Education is a serious problem for the parents of these children.

—Will it be better to send the children to a local school and let them have an American education?

—Is it better to send them to a Japanese school to continue their education in Japanese because they will be in America for only three years?

—Should the children and their mother stay in Japan?

Unfortunately this problem will not be solved for quite a while.

---

*Tetsuko Kuroyanagi: a very popular actress/entertainer

*Totto-chan: a character in one of Ms. Kuroyanagi's books describing her own childhood

What can be done for now is to expand the size of the Japanese school so that it can take all the applicants. But even a seemingly simple thing like that is not easily carried out. Many people in Japan seem to think, not knowing the agony of the parents, that Japanese children living in New York or London should go to a local school, believing it will be a wonderful opportunity for them to learn English and absorb Western culture.

Two rental cars driven by former *kikokushijo* (returnees)* came to a small bay. The smooth surface of the water was shining in the sun like a mirror. "This must be the Lake of Shining Waters in *Anne of Green Gables!*" my wife exclaimed, overcome with emotion.

A Hungarian Woman Named Maria

There is a bronze statue of a nude boy in downtown Budapest. The boy's penis caught my eye because it was uncircumcized. Ghassan, the Lebanese colleague I was with, gave me a slow nod. His large Middle Eastern eyes shine when he is in a good mood. "Why did you nod at me?" I asked him, and he said, "You were thinking about circumcision, weren't you?" I was a little taken aback by his having read my mind.

According to Ghassan, in the old days when no anesthetic was available, father, brothers, and male friends held a boy's limbs while a village expert carried out the circumcision. The mere thought of it gives me a shudder. When the pain subsides after about three weeks the boy will enjoy opening a lot of presents he is given for the occasion. Ghassan says it gives the boys a great pleasure, and I add for my part, "Also you can enjoy the feeling of becoming an adult."

**kikokushijo:* a recently-evolved term to describe children returning to Japan from long periods of residence abroad

In America, when boys are born, doctors recommend circumcision immediately. It is not a must, but because it is inconvenient to be uncircumcized as an adult, almost every parent agrees to the operation. Should there be a realistic modern statue of a naked boy in America, it would undoubtedly have a smaller version of a grown man's penis. Such was the discussion Ghassan and I had quietly, so that our young Hungarian guide Maria would not hear us.

I find Hungarian women attractive. They appear to be European on first glance, but with a closer look they appear Slavic. With blue eyes and fair skin, they have the simple and ingenuous beauty of the ladylike women of generations ago. My eyes have grown accustomed to American women who diet endlessly, wishing to be like skinny, suntanned models, and it makes my heart fill with nostalgia to see a full, rounded, fair-skinned woman. Maria wore her hair long, so long that it almost reached her bottom. With an amber comb in her dark brown hair, and virtually no makeup except for a light lipstick, and with such mesmerizing large blue eyes . . . Maria, oh, what a graceful, elegant woman.

The hilly side of the city is called Buda and the flat side Pest, and in between the Danube River flows. Budapest was one of the capitals of the Austro-Hungarian Empire. The city, which was called the Paris of Eastern Europe in those days, still retains its beauty. It makes you feel as though you have been brought back to medieval Europe by a time machine. The beauty and characteristics of the city were perhaps maintained because it was in the Eastern Bloc after World War II.

Maria took us to the Parliament building on the river bank. It is a majestic construction in neo-baroque style and it was the largest building in the world in the late nineteenth century. On the way to the Parliament, when Maria said, pointing at a seemingly ordinary street, "This is where our parents fought," I felt my body stiffen. Budapest experienced street fighting and occupation by Nazi Germany, and upheaval again in 1956. The buildings there still have visible bullet marks.

Maria's "parents" must be about my age. I was studying in America at the time of upheaval in 1956. Some ten Hungarians came to our dormitory, claiming that they were refugees from Hungary, and they stayed on. I never gave a serious thought then about what they had done, but they were the brave people who risked their lives and fought against their authoritarian state before fleeing to America.

Hungary was founded in 896 by Magyars. Ever since then the nation repeatedly suffered invasion and occupation. It is located in the center of Europe and has the riches of its plains and the Danube valley, which was perhaps the reason for the series of invasions. In the thirteenth century it was occupied by the Huns, and in the sixteenth century by Ottoman Turkey.

Hungary finally liberated itself from Soviet oppression. It took a turn of 180 degrees from socialism to capitalism. But for some reason they do not use the word capitalism. Instead they call it market economy. The University of Economics in Budapest was called until recently Karl Marx University. The students there studied Marx's *Das Kapital,* so they cannot use the word "capitalism" now.

I came to know a Japanese man who works for a major Japanese securities firm. He told me that in the late 1960s, as a graduate student at University of Tokyo, he was active in the student movement. Because he devoted himself to Marx he did not think that anyone would want to hire him. But he got a job at a securities firm and it has been three years since he came to Eastern Europe. "Did you really read the whole of Marx's *Das Kapital?*" I asked him. He said proudly, "Yes, of course. I learned the first ten pages almost by heart . When I debated with the elite of the Soviet Communist Party, I won the argument. I don't think any other man has perused the book as closely as I."

When I was a student in Japan, Marxism was the mainstream,

and modern economics was a byway. Now, few students study Marx, and only professors still believe in it. Maria said, grinning, "Hungary has certainly changed to capitalism, but it is capitalism without capital."

There was a cement enclosure in the corner of the park with a hot spring in it. People were enjoying soaking themselves in the water. It is considered to be effective for rheumatism.

The Shy Smile of Chopin's Country

Politicians have a different manner from non-politicians. Even the suave and polite Mr. Noboru Takeshita sometimes reveals piercing eyes.

I saw President Bush yesterday from only five or six meters away, and his firm but animated face gave me the impression that he was not an ordinary person.

The politicians I met in Warsaw, without exception, did not look very much like politicians. The night we arrived in Warsaw from Budapest a politician invited us to a dinner. He looked like Jesus Christ with his thin body, beard, and clear eyes. In the middle of the dinner he stood up and said "Please excuse me, but I have promised to take my son to see Akira Kurosawa's *Kumonosujo* (Spider's Castle?)." Polish people are fond of movies. They tell me that most of Kurosawa's movies have been shown in Poland dubbed in Polish.

Polish-Americans, both men and women, are all good-looking. In Poland I saw the reason for that. The children especially are adorable.

For forty years Poland was under Soviet oppression. They finally won democracy and are enjoying their freedom—but no, I do not want to look at it in such a stereotyped way. I want to see with my own eyes, without any prejudiced preconception or empathy, the real life of Polish people. I want to see an ordinary

Polish home, if possible, and to meet ordinary citizens. It was with such thoughts that I came to Warsaw.

A Finance Ministry man in his mid-30s named Marian took care of me. His English was not fluent but it was accurate, and he spoke very slowly. I could tell that he thought first in his own language and then translated his thoughts into English. I do the same. Misery makes strange bedfellows.

Marian cried, "It's Copernicus!" and we asked the driver to stop. There was a large bronze statue of Copernicus holding a globe in his hands. I took a long look at the statue, reminding myself that he was a great man. It must have been truly sensational when he introduced the theory that the earth revolved on its axis, when everyone else believed that the sun revolved around the earth. Marian appeared pleased to see me looking at the statue and nodded to myself.

The Poles are also proud of Chopin. There is a statue of him in the park on Ujazdowskie Avenue. "Some Japanese wanted to buy the statue but we wouldn't sell it," Marian muttered.

I noticed a facial expression that was common among Polish people. They smile shyly, twisting their lips, which is an expression never seen in Americans. Americans are not shy. They do not hesitate, but are simple, clear-cut, outspoken, and straightforward.

It has been so long since I came to America that I habitually think that Caucasians are Americans. But in Poland I saw Caucasians who, although physically like Americans, smiled shyly and put on a look of hesitation, which I had never seen before. It was a great discovery. I do not know if their long history made them like that or if it is because they remain skeptical even after their liberation from socialism. I was surprised to see for the first time melancholic expressions on Caucasian faces, but at the same time I felt relieved to see human warmth.

Marian asked me to stop by his apartment. I wondered if he was trying to be accommodating because I had earlier mentioned my desire to see the life of ordinary Poles. I graciously declined the invitation, but he was persistent. I finally accepted on condition that he not offer me any hospitality. He smiled and went to a public phone to call his wife, I assumed, to inform her of an unexpected visitor.

It was nearly six o'clock in the evening. Marian and I got into a car. On the way to his apartment, we heard a siren, and a motorcade of some ten cars went past us. I caught just a glimpse of former President Ronald Reagan, who looked well. I did not see Nancy Reagan. Perhaps she was in another car.

The building where Marian lived was four stories high, and looked very much like early apartment buildings of the Housing Corporation in Tokyo. Marian lived on the ground floor (the first floor) with his wife, eight-year-old daughter, and five-year-old son.

When the door opened I saw his wife, Yolanda, a dazzling beauty just like a Hollywood star, dressed in bright green. Beside her were two children gazing at me as if they were looking at an alien from another planet. Their faces said that they had never seen an Oriental before.

Marian's two-bedroom apartment was about 60 yd^2 (540 ft^2). On the dining table were a homemade cake and some tea. Beside the table was a "gramophone" and some records. There was also an old-fashioned 10-inch television set. The green dress Yolanda wore had puffed sleeves and a flared skirt, just like the ones Mieko Takamine* used to wear in her movies in the old days. The little boy, George, inched himself toward me as he became less shy. Mary, their daughter, showed me many of her crayon drawings.

The window looked out on a playground. "It's dinner time," I heard a mother calling to her children playing there. It was a sight I was familiar with as a child growing up in Japan.

---

*Mieko Takamine: actress popular in 1950s.

Mary gave me her drawing of tulips. I kissed her on the cheek and she twisted her body shyly.

Brandenburg

The light of Paris began to come into view as the plane descended. My spirits began to rise.

I love Paris. Nearly thirty years ago when I stepped onto the soil of Paris for the first time in my life, I trembled with excitement. Prices are high, Parisians are not kind to people who do not speak French, and sometimes you do experience unpleasantness. Despite all that, I love the city.

I studied French at the university as a second foreign language, although I cannot speak the language at all now; I like French modern literature, and I had a French friend when I was studying in Philadelphia—perhaps these are factors contributing to my affinity towards France.

The taxi driver drove like a maniac, like the kamikaze taxi drivers of Tokyo a decade ago. I was so scared that I had my eyes closed all the way to my hotel. Chris Bellinger of MIGA, who had arrived in Paris earlier, was waiting for me in the hotel lobby. Chris is French-American and speaks fluent French. "Last night the unification of Germany took place. I wonder what French people think of it," I said to him. Chris, who is in his mid-30s, replied, fondling his luxuriant moustache with his right index finger, "As a European, I am happy for them, but at the same time, a unified Germany will be extremely strong, and I fear that it may pose a threat to France, like before."

European history has been a series of terrible confrontations and blood-letting. In particular, French people must remember vividly the fear and hatred they felt toward Nazi Germany. I wonder if they are now more concerned about the probability of a unified Germany taking the leading role in the integration of the EC in 1993, which the French had thought was theirs. I did not want to torment the kind-hearted Chris with further cross-questioning, so I said "Bon soir," and parted.

On October 2, 1990, at 11:30 at night, I had my eyes fixed on the television in my hotel room in Barcelona. I tried all the channels and found one in English, but it was airing a women's golf tournament. I chose a channel showing Brandenburg in Berlin. A female newscaster in a yellow suit and an elderly male colleague with the collar of his raincoat turned up, were rattling away in Spanish. "11:55:00" came on the screen. It is eleven o'clock, 55 minutes, 00 seconds. The numbers changed—tic, tic, tic. It must be their intention to show this historic occasion second by second. I hear the word "momento" repeatedly. They must be exclaiming "The moment in the century that is going to make history is about to arrive." I wished I was in Japan so that I could listen to the commentary in Japanese. But on the other hand, Berlin and Barcelona are in the same time zone, and being in the same continent as the city where the historic moment was about to come, I was able to feel a "realism" I could not have felt in Japan.

Suddenly I wondered what sorts of productions world television would air on December 31, 2000, at 11:59:59, when in a second the world will celebrate the end of the twentieth century and the beginning of the twenty-first. I wonder if they have already started planning programs for the occasion. It is still many years away. I will be seventy then. I wonder if I will still be alive and well then.

An hour earlier my colleagues had celebrated my fifty-ninth birthday one day too early in Barcelona. I was to turn fifty-nine on October 3, 1990. They made the excuse that although it was October 2 in Barcelona it was already October 3 in Japan. My colleagues in MIGA with whom I was on a mission were: Boris (a Yugoslav in his mid-40s), Yuzuna (a Burmese, Boris's wife, a graduate of Sophia University, a petite lady who looked completely Japanese), and Leigh (an American in his early 50s with the air of a university professor). We were having Japanese food for dinner, when I unintentionally mentioned "By Japanese time, it is already my fifty-ninth birthday." After a while Yuzuna asked to be excused as if she was going to the ladies' room, and then in a short while Boris followed. I thought it was rather strange because Americans or Europeans seldom leave the table during a meal. Then it struck me that they must be planning to throw a birthday party for me. I was slightly sorry that I had said it was my birthday.

They took me to a fancy confectioner with glass cases full of scrumptious looking chocolates and cakes. The background music was Beethoven's *Symphony No. 9.* There was a tea room in the back. We sat at the table by the window. An elderly waiter in a white shirt and a bow tie brought a cake to our table. The number 59 was formed with red candles on a chocolate cake that still looked warm. I blew out the two slender candles next to the number, while Yuzuna took some pictures. The three of them quietly sang, "Happy birthday to you, . . ." I ate my birthday cake, surrounded by a Yugoslav, a Burmese, and an American, listening to Beethoven's *Ninth* in Barcelona.

A Renowned Picture in Bonn

The expression "absent-minded professor" refers to unusually clever people whose minds are remote from their immediate surroundings. They almost always forget their umbrellas, or they bump into utility poles, walking deep in thought. It is a phenomenon often seen among scholars and writers.

Jurgen was a typical "absent-minded professor," although he was an able man with a Ph.D. in law. In the spring of 1990, Jurgen and I went to Paris to attend a MIGA seminar there. Jurgen was a legal advisor to MIGA and he always accompanied me to such seminars. As he was taking care of the procedures of airline check-ins, he kept my air tickets. At the end of the seminar, Jurgen gave me back my tickets because I was going on to Madrid and Jurgen to Geneva, and I returned to my hotel. I was packing in my hotel room when Jurgen, who was supposed to be in Geneva then, came in. "Sorry, I made a mistake," he pulled some air tickets out of his pocket and held them out to me. He had given me his tickets by mistake and did not realize it until he arrived at the airport. I had no intention of accusing him of a careless mistake. I simply could not help but laugh that he had done it again. Needless to say, he had to delay his trip to Geneva by one day.

I once traveled to Istanbul with Jurgen. We were invited to a dinner by the Finance Minister at seven o'clock in Merhaba, according to Jurgen. Traffic was heavy in the evening in Istanbul. When we realized it was already six-thirty, we hurried downstairs and picked up a taxi in front of the hotel. The taxi driver, skillfully maneuvering through tortuous and crowded streets, headed for the suburbs. After about 30 minutes the taxi stopped in front of a small restaurant by the shore. It was an extremely shabby-looking house. I was quite dubious: would a finance minister invite his guests to such a seedy place? We asked a moustached man in the restaurant who appeared to be a maitre d'hotel but he simply kept shaking his head. We had no alternative but to go back to the taxi. Jurgen yelled at the driver in his English with a German accent, but the driver just kept shrugging his shoulders. Another 30-minute drive took us to a restaurant on the corner of a main street, which was packed with young people in jeans, and was deafeningly noisy with jazz music from a jukebox. I was certain that this could not be the place. I did not even get out of the taxi and asked the driver to take us back to the hotel. Both Jurgen and I were exhausted by then, having been irritated for over one hour. Where on earth was Merhaba? To double-check, we asked a hotel bellboy. "It's on the second floor of this hotel," hc replied unconcernedly. It was the "Merhaba Room," just like the "Heian Room" or the "Kasuga Room" in hotels in Japan. The Finance Minister received us with a smile despite our delay of over one hour, and greeted us with "Merhaba." Merhaba can mean "Hello" or "Thank you" in Turkish, and is a greeting word with multiple meanings similar to the Hawaiian "Aloha."

The next day we visited Bonn. Because Germany was Jurgen's country, I had no worries whatsoever. After dinner we decided to go for a sauna in our hotel. We took a shower and then in the nude went into a hot, dry sauna room. "You worked hard today as usual," I thanked Jurgen and closed my eyes. It was warm there and I felt indescribably good. Then I sensed that someone had come in. I opened my eyes to find, to my astonishment, two women. For a moment I scrupulously studied their two naked bodies with a scientist's eye. They were a girl of about 15 or 16 years of age with a mature body and an innocent looking face, and a round, middle-aged woman who appeared to be the girl's mother. I gazed absorbedly at the two women as if I was appreciating a renowned picture by a European artist. Then I looked at Jurgen. My eyes must have had a reproachful look that suggested he had taken me to a women's sauna by mistake. He glared back at me with his large eyes and said, "Saunas in Germany are mixed."

We were strolling along the lake in Zurich, when Jurgen said "I went into my mother's room to tell her that the breakfast was ready. But she didn't make the slightest move. She had had a heart attack. She was as fit as a fiddle until the day before . . ." Jurgen was then a student at a university in California. His mother had come to visit him from Germany, and had been pleased to see his dormitory room neat and tidy despite her expectation of its being otherwise. She stayed in a nearby motel, in a large suite with two bedrooms and a kitchen. Jurgen, pleased by his mother's praise for his tidiness, had crept into the kitchen so as not to wake his mother and prepared a breakfast of toast, fresh orange juice, and tea.

"You never know when death will visit you," Jurgen said with a clouded face. He has left MIGA to work for the EC in Brussels.

A Bride in Bangkok

It was cold with a sign of sleet when I left Washington. I boarded the plane with the collar of my trench coat turned up and my hands in my pockets. When I arrived in Bangkok in the evening, I smelled the air of the south. It was lukewarm and the fragrance of flowers was mixed with the smell of food.

My room is in the Oriental Hotel overlooking the Chao Phraya river. The doorman is a tall Indian, and the glass door is opened graciously by two bellboys every time someone goes in or out. There is a counter by the elevator door on each floor and two bellboys are stationed there at all times. Walk along the carpeted corridor to your room and a bellboy swiftly arrives at the door before you to open it with a master key. Request a morning call at seven, and at seven o'clock sharp a cheerful woman's voice wakes you up with "Good morning." This much may not be so different from any other hotels, but at the Oriental Hotel they ring you again five minutes later to make sure that you have woken up.

The purpose of my trip to Bangkok was to invite the Government of Thailand to join MIGA. Industrialized nations such as the U.S., Japan, and European countries make quite a lot of investments in Thailand. Some investors wish to insure their investments through MIGA. But it cannot be done because Thailand is not a member. There are Thai businessmen who invest directly in the countries of Africa or South America. They seek a guarantee from MIGA to protect their investments from political risks, but we cannot comply with these requests either because Thailand is not a member of MIGA. The World Bank currently has 155 member countries, 99 of which have joined MIGA. We would like to persuade the other 56 countries to sign, so as to have all the 155 countries join MIGA. Among the ASEAN countries—Thailand, Malaysia, the Philippines, Indonesia, Singapore, and Brunei—so far only Indonesia and the Philippines have signed.

The Oriental Hotel is located a little away from the center of the city. I used to visit Bangkok two or three times a year when I was working at Nomura Securities Headquarters during 1978 and 1979. The purpose of my trips then was to persuade the Finance Ministry of Thailand to issue national bonds in yen in Japan. I stayed at a downtown hotel on those visits. But once, in the spring of 1979, I stayed at the Oriental Hotel. Their bathrobe was very much to my liking. It was something between *yukata** and Judo wear, and had a sash sewn in. I find it too tiresome to put on pajamas with a top and pants, and the yukata style sleepwear Japanese hotels provide is not very comfortable. The bathrobe of the Oriental is 100% cotton and feels pleasant against the skin. And because it has a sash around the waist it is very convenient. The bathrobe was almost perfect sleepwear for me. I purchased one in 1979 and was using it until recently. I was at a loss what to do when it was finally too worn out to be used any longer. I even thought of writing to the Oriental to ask them to send me one. But I decided it was too much trouble, and so I had two bathrobes made to order by a shirtmaker in Washington. They were reasonably satisfactory, but still it was not the same, and they did not give me total satisfaction.

I was delighted to find the same robe today in my room. The difference from the 1979 one is that the new one has a pocket on the left breast. I do not know why a bathrobe needs a pocket. I

**yukata:* a lightweight cotton kimono used sometimes as a sleeping robe purchased two robes before I forgot and packed them in my suitcase.

The daytime temperature in Bangkok goes up at least to 30°C (86°F), so when you enter the air-conditioned hotel lobby it feels cool, and makes you feel relieved. Just like the lobbies of the Imperial or New Otani Hotels in Tokyo, the lobby of the Dusit Thani Hotel, which is located in the middle of the business district, is extremely crowded.

Thailand has a population of many different races, including many people of Chinese, Indian, and Burmese descent. In addition, there are many tourists from Europe, America, Australia, and Japan. The hotel lobby is a melting pot of races.

Tonight, a wedding reception is being held in the largest ballroom of the hotel. I was invited to the reception along with Ghassan El-Rifai of MIGA. About twenty young women dressed in folk costumes of bright blue and red are receiving guests at the door. On the receiving line the bride is in a wedding dress of pure white and the groom in a tuxedo. Thais greet others with a graceful *wai*—with their hands put together, like Japanese people when they pray in front of God or Buddha. They bring their hands very close to their nose, instead of shaking hands like Americans or bowing like Japanese. Some people actually touch their noses with their hands. Women slightly bend their knees as they put their hands together. It looks extremely graceful.

The father of the groom is a wealthy man in Thailand, and 1,800 guests—including leading figures of the political and financial worlds—attended the reception. The bride changed her dress to a Thai folk costume. A prominent figure in the political world who was formerly a deputy prime minister proposed a toast. The guests were becoming carried away crying "Chaiyo, chaiyo, chaiyo." "Chaiyo" seems to mean "Banzai." A "consummation ceremony" follows the reception. Rose petals are scattered all over the bed on which ceramic male and female cats are placed. Cats belong to the house. Even if they wander quite far away they always come back. Perhaps the cats signify the bride's prayer that the groom will never stray far from their home.

The bride is Japanese. The bride and groom had met each other in America as students. They looked very happy.

Part Three

Back in Japan

8

Fitting Back In

Retire to America? Yes, but. . .

I arrived in New York at the end of January with seven large suitcases, which a porter carried from the customs area to a car parked quite far away. For a second, I wondered how much to tip him. It used to be fifty cents per bag but I figured it must be higher now. I settled on fifteen dollars, thinking that the equivalent of two thousand or so Japanese yen would be reasonable enough. The porter seemed happy. Not only did he thank me he added "very much!"

As I write this in New York, I am conscious that the yen has appreciated considerably, even at close to 130 yen to the dollar. Convert what one pays for meals, clothes, or a taxi into yen and suddenly prices in the U.S. appear quite a bit cheaper. In Tokyo, an 8,000 yen muskmelon, a 30,000 yen French dinner, and a finely tailored 300,000 yen suit are incredibly expensive by any standard. I might seriously consider retiring in America if the yen goes to 100 per dollar, and if the inflation, interest, and growth rates remain more or less at their present levels.

Just imagine. Suppose I had ¥200 million at retirement. At an exchange rate of one-hundred yen to the dollar. This would convert to $2 million. With $400,000, I could buy a house in, for example, the suburbs of San Francisco. I could keep $100,000 in cash and invest $1.5 million in 30-year Treasury Bonds. With a yield of 9 percent, I would have an annual income of $135,000 for the next thirty years. Out of that, I could put $35,000 in the bank for a rainy day. This would leave me with $100,000. Six thousand a month would be plenty to support my wife and myself, so $72,000 a year should be enough. We could use the remaining $28,000 to take annual trips, once to Japan and once to Europe. Or maybe we could visit Japan twice. We would have $14,000 or ¥1.4 million to spend on each trip. Assume that a round-trip air ticket to Japan for two would cost around ¥400,000. We could spend ¥80,000 a day for ten days and still be left with pocket money of about ¥200,000! All this is still a dream and I will probably not go through with it, but. . .

If I ever settle permanently in America, I would miss *rakugo* and *kouta* lessons. And, ah! the Tokyo Giants ball games and Konishiki and the sumo wrestling grand championships and my alma mater Waseda University rugby games—too many things I could not do without. Then there are the NHK television weekly drama series and occasionally Sachiko Kobayashi's spirited *enka* songs. I would want to see my children and grandchildren often and play a relaxing game of golf or mahjong with close friends. By that age, I would also want to be free of my endless struggle with English. I expect to happily "fade away," surrounded by my family in my sweet little home in Japan . . . even if the yen appreciates to fifty yen to the dollar.

Illicit love: Japan vs. America

Our twenty-one year old daughter who is studying art in New York saw the movie "Fatal Attraction" and urged me to see it. The story is apparently about a married man who had an extramarital affair which ended in disaster. The obvious moral is that if you play with fire, you'll get burned.

According to my daughter, married women in New York are taking their husbands to see it as a harsh warning. I am not sure she knows what she is talking about. At twenty-one, she may fool people that she is an independent-minded adult managing by herself in New York City, but to me she is still a child. From a Japanese point of view, if the film has such a terrible ending, respectable housewives would be unlikely to take their husbands. The title is suggestive enough to attract interest, but I presume that most Japanese men would see it alone, as would most of their wives. Then, they would not admit to seeing it, but continue with their married lives as if nothing had happened. Such is the way of married couples in Japan. My daughter must have heard the story from one of her friends, but it cannot be representative of all married women in New York; anyway, she is far too young to understand the complexities of the husband/wife relationship.

Maintaining the Status Quo

A relationship between a husband and a wife is a private matter. This is so whether in America or in Japan. In America, even older couples call each other "honey," or "my dear," and publically hug and kiss each other. It may be just a habit, but I think there is much more to it. To demonstrate affection in public, they have to love each other. If a marriage is cold, few Americans would feign such affection.

Is there a difference between Japan and America in the areas of conjugal love? If asked, I would probably say yes, after some thought. Being a man, I can at least appreciate the difference between Japanese and American men. The most pointed difference is that American men are more "earnest."

I recall doing laundry every Saturday during my student days at the University of Pennsylvania. My roommates, Tom and George, were good at taking care of their laundry. They would roll up their briefs, pat their socks flat and put them neatly away in their drawers. It was almost a pleasure to watch them systematically go about their chores, sometimes even humming a tune.

I also think of those Friday evenings when American men haul all sorts of gear into their station wagons, and drive their families for three hours to their weekend houses in the country. There are few American men who idle away the whole day in front of a television set. Even fewer American men, at least in my experience, resign themselves to the status quo or simply couldn't care less.

In Japan, divorce is infrequent because most Japanese men are discouraged from even thinking about the tedious divorce procedure. As a result, Japanese men prefer to maintain the status quo, a preference that applies equally to employment and marriage. Once a commitment is made, they prefer to be philosophical about it and would rather keep things as they are than bother to change them.

Changing the Present Situation

I have heard that the divorce rate in America is very high. I do not know how they calculate the rate, but it is certainly quite high. Unlike the Japanese, American men prefer to change their situations in order to be happy in marriage as well as in their careers.

In an essay I wrote sometime ago, called "Men of Wall Street," I referred, with some degree of envy, to two happily remarried American couples. Half a year later, when my essays were published in book form, *(Wall Street Diary),* both happy couples were already divorced.

People have love affairs everywhere in the world, in America, as well as in China, the Soviet Union, or wherever humans live, for that matter. In America, it may be quite difficult to maintain such an affair for two or three years. First of all, the woman would refuse to resign herself to being "the other woman." A series of secret rendezvous would work, at most, for a year or so.

After that, she would want the relationship to receive public endorsement. If she received an invitation to a party, she would want her man to accompany her.

An American man, unlike a Japanese man, has the courage to undergo the complicated procedures of divorce. Thus, lovers end up being formally married and, as a consequence, the divorce rate naturally becomes high. An affair in America may start out as secret relationship between already married partners, but eventually it evolves into a prologue for the next marriage.

I recall having read in an essay by Naoya Uchimura, a playwright, about his struggle to find the appropriate words to say to his wife on his deathbed. In English "I love you" would say it all. But no suitable expression exists in Japanese. Uchimura through about this for some time and at last decided that he would say: "I am a lucky man to have had you as my wife." Pleased with himself he celebrated the night with a glass of wine. Would that be an American type of ending? That is, would he be able to say "I'm lucky I found you" after trying many times to find his true love? Or would it be the Japanese way? Putting an end to both a long affair and an equally long, unhappy marriage? When he said, "I am lucky it was you," what he really meant was "Only you could have been so forgiving and patient. I appreciate your being good to me during all this time, when I have been unfaithful to you." Whether in Japan or America, every relationship between man and wife is unique.

Oriental Patience

You have probably seen the film "Wall Street." Well, I found out that Wall Street really *does* have the sort of atmosphere depicted in the film. Naturally, a movie has its exaggerations and its omissions, but the film is frightfully powerful. In almost two hours, it succeeded in creating a definite image. Wall Street has of course, its share of people chasing money. There are big fish, small fish, and thousands of monsters. One April evening, I was having dinner with the writer of the script, Kenneth Lipper. He assured me that there were no role models for his film. Nonetheless the SEC (Securities and Exchange Commission) conducted an investigation involving insider trading. And Lipper had met the suspect, Ivan Boesky, simply out of interest. Lipper asked Boesky why he had taken such risks when he had made enough money to last his lifetime; a simple question, perhaps, but one that would interest an ordinary person. Apparently Boesky just grinned and said nothing. Lipper concluded that making money was Boesky's method of ego building.

When people buy stocks they want to make money. Stocks sometimes make money and sometimes lose money. We all know that much, at least theoretically. But we like to think that somehow we will always make money. On Wall Street, people say that stocks require the patience of the Oriental. Americans know that they are often hot-tempered and easily thrown out of control. They remind themselves that a little Oriental patience is a good thing to have. Their definition of Oriental, however, does not include Japanese. To them, Oriental means Chinese. In the eyes of the Americans, the Japanese, who are forever wanting to emulate the West, are not pure Orientals. I am afraid to say that Americans see us as impatient, shrewd, and canny people to watch out for.

A New Image of Husband and Wife, a Young Bride's Attitude

Recently, two of my close friends' daughters were married, one after the other. Both fathers, like myself, were born in 1931, and since I have three unmarried daughters myself, I intently watched my friends during the wedding parties, trying to discern the emotions of the fathers of the brides. I was somewhat surprised that they both looked fine throughout the ceremony. Maybe it is not the wedding day, but the preceding days that are sad.

The brides at both weddings were calmer and cooler than their fathers. They looked fully prepared and had rather dignified attitudes. Both women are college graduates and hold professional jobs.

Their bosses spoke at their weddings and both said: "My congratulations on your wedding. But I have one request for the groom. Please don't tell your bride to quit her job." This was no mere compliment. Both of my friends' daughters are bilingual in Japanese and English, and are professionals in their specialties. Their employers would suffer if they were to quit.

Women Students Ruin the Country was the shocking title of a book by a Waseda University professor about twenty years ago. While male students enter a university determined to study seriously, the author said, female students merely want the "college graduate" title to enrich their "trousseau." The point of the book was that the state and universities totally wasted money on such women students.

In the past, all a bride had to do was to endure the wedding ceremony, her head lowered, her face overly made-up to have a frozen lack of expression, and her hair covered by an ornate headdress. Modern-day brides, in contrast, laugh at the speeches and actively participate. Times have changed for the better, I thought. Soon, perhaps, a book entitled *Women Students Bring Prosperity to the Nation* will be published.

Husband and Wife at the Center

Although it is hard to generalize, it seems that young people today seek a partner with whom they can talk freely. Due to economic reasons, sometimes both spouses work. But I wonder whether a husband today may want to confine his wife to housework and child-rearing. Maybe men now prefer their wives to have jobs, contact with society, and opinions of their own. Wouldn't that make discussions much more interesting?

Most of my business acquaintances on Wall Street were from double-income families. Even after a couple has a child, the wife continues working, and a nanny looks after their child(ren). Interestingly, household help is cheaper and more readily available in New York than in Tokyo, probably because the labor market is more liberalized in New York.

I used to wonder where I could find an 'ordinary' family, meaning one where the wife cares for the children and the home, while the husband works. Of course, Wall Street is not typical America. In the United States, not just in the country but in a small regional city, you can find many "ordinary" families. Life in the U.S. certainly centers around the husband and wife. Culture itself stems from the couple.

Patience

Many people in Tokyo push the "Close" button as soon as they get in an elevator, though the doors will automatically close in about ten seconds. In companies, you see women employees trotting from one department to another carrying documents, even when they are not urgent. I guess those feel impatient and constantly on edge.

It may be a coincidence, but many Japanese businesses have set up shop in Bangkok, and now, after a while, even the leisurely Thais, have started to push the "Close" button. I've also heard that people wait in line for two days to buy tickets for the Wimbledon tennis tournament. I saw them on TV, calmly and quietly waiting their turn. Japanese in a similar situation would be seething with anger.

At New York department stores, sales people just ring up the bill and give you the merchandise. If you want it wrapped, you have to go to a different section. And there, again, you often find ten customers ahead of you, patiently waiting in line. If you want to ask a sales person a simple question such as "Do you accept credit cards?" you won't get an answer until the customer before you has been served. Salespersons concentrate only on the matter at hand.

Whenever I accompany visitors from Japan to department stores in New York, I forewarn them that service is not as quick as in Japan. Nevertheless, I end up muttering apologies as their impatience clearly shows when confronted with the reality of New York. It seems that you have to wait for everything in understaffed, advanced countries. Japan may soon end up the same way.

My Country, Japan

I am positive that people are most comfortable in their own native countries. That, of course, assumes that one's homeland is a comfortable place to live in.

Exactly one year ago, I returned to Japan after sixteen years in New York. Since then, acquaintances from New York have commented that I've gained weight or that I look much less stern than I did on Wall Street. I interpret such comments to mean that I have lost the tension I had in New York and have become relaxed and somewhat flabby.

While in New York, I quit drinking, and gave up smoking. I swam each and every morning. I followed a cholesterol-conscious diet. As a result, I stoically grumbled about what an uninteresting man I had become.

I used to read the *New York Times* and the *Wall Street Journal* every morning on my way to work. When I lifted my eyes from the papers, I could see on my left the Brooklyn Bridge, New

York's prettiest, and on my right the skyscrapers of Wall Street. The next time a Japanese TV company sends a crew over to shoot Wall Street footage, I will recommend this picturesque view.

I got into the habit of interrupting my reading to look at that scene as I passed. I always felt a slight excitement, almost like a warrior's anxiety before a battle. My heart beat as I told myself, "I am off to the battlefield again." Not exactly a sense of tragic heroism, but rather a resigned courage, to help me face problems as they come.

We had an internal meeting every morning at 8:30, with two representatives from each section. The conference table, with only thirty seats, was usually full. When financial markets fall, the chief executive should look all the more calm and confident. Or maybe he should be serious to tighten up the atmosphere. To tell the truth, I am not quite sure which is better, though I personally prefer to smile.

In a similar situation in Japan, I would give a pep talk with words such as: "We are facing tough times. I urge everyone to batten down the hatches." But it is rather hard to give this sort of speech in English. Even with a perfect translation, I doubt the speech would win any audience support. Americans are not easily convinced with abstract expressions.

Our meetings were attended by the cream of the crop of Wall Street businessmen—smart graduates of Harvard and Yale. Each person had a distinct character and brimmed with confidence. I always felt at a loss over what kind of pep talk to give to such a group.

American professional groups in general are not devoted to the idea of striving "for the team." Most Wall Street pros are like baseball players on a one or two-year contract. Fixed salaries are rare, and most earn commissions according to the amount of business they generate. They work like crazy, but it is hard to say whether they do it for the company or for themselves. One does not encounter this difficulty in Japan.

In Japan, the whole company occasionally goes on an overnight trip to a hot-spring resort, where they all wear the same kimonos, and drink up a storm. In the U.S., such group behavior would be unthinkable under any circumstances.

The *Philadelphia Bulletin* newspaper had a famous slogan: "Nearly Everybody Reads the Bulletin." "Nearly everybody," that is, not "everybody" but "very close to everybody reads this paper."

Life in Japan is based on the assuring feeling that "nearly everybody" thinks and does the same things. Everything somehow goes smoothly day after day based on this assumption.

Until Admiral Perry landed in Uraga with his black ships in 1853, the Japanese led a quiet, solitary life with no outside contact. Even today, Japan may still long to be left alone, but we can't get away with it any more. The country has become too wealthy economically.

The world no longer considers Japan a "mysterious land in the exotic East." People have an unfortunate general tendency to gloat over the misfortune of others and to envy their good fortune. This tendency applies to both individuals and countries. In those countries not as well-off, people now look to Japan with envy, jealousy, and bitterness, which is a distorted view about this newly wealthy country. Japan cares little about such perceptions, and continues to cling to its time-honored "village" mentality.

A series of mercilessly competitive entrance examinations starts at age four or five in order to screen children for admission into privileged elementary schools. At such an early age, the desire to catch the "elite train" is instilled within the Japanese people. The bureaucrats, graduates of the University of Tokyo, guide the able and hard-working citizens, and steer the country on a set course. Regardless of whether the yen is strong or weak, our people are always focused on the nation and unite with excitement at such group slogans as "let's achieve 100 million such-and-such."

The little "village" has nothing to worry about. Living in the paradise of Japan, one need not be concerned about such things as being attacked while riding the subway late at night, or the frighteningly diverse ways of thinking of people in other cultures. The Japanese businessmen fight these problems even as I write not only in New York, but all over the world.

Come to think of it, I'm enjoying a peaceful life in my comfortable homeland, that mysterious Japan. Maybe it's true. Maybe I do have plump cheeks and a calmer outlook.

9

A Diary of the Campaign

May 24, 1992 (Sunday)

I played golf with an old college friend at Tama Country Club, but I was so occupied with my scheduled meeting tonight with Morihiro Hosokawa, leader of the new minority party called the Japan New Party (JNP), that I played a lousy game.

At 6:30 PM, I arrived at the hotel he was staying at. I went up to his room and pressed the doorbell outside his door, and Mr. Hosokawa himself answered the door and let me in. He is rather tall. In the room there was a small living room area where we sat.

In Japan, when you want to have an advantageous position in an important discussion like this, it is usually better to sit back and let the other person begin speaking first. But this is impossible unless you have a great deal of composure. When sitting across the table from someone, if they make you feel pressured, your nerves race ahead with impatience and all of a sudden you find yourself speaking first.

This evening, Mr. Hosokawa just sat there quietly, looking for all the world as though he had nothing in particular to say. Unwittingly, I fell right into his well-laid trap. This must be how it feels when you meet your favorite movie star, I thought. Mr. Hosokawa continued to look intently at me, with his large eyes sparkling in a broad smile. When my cup became empty, he leisurely picked up the teapot and gracefully poured me some more tea.

Even though I had not drunk a drop of alcohol, my face was all red and flushed. I could feel the breeze blowing against it as I left the hotel.

Just before I left, Mr. Hosokawa suddenly said, "I want you to run for Senator (elected member of the Upper House of the Japanese Diet) on the JNP ticket," but I felt that I would never be able to do anything like that. (If I could only contain my excitement I would surely regain my composure and become my old self again, I thought.)

I am scheduled to return to Washington tomorrow; if I go back there, I will certainly recover from this feeling of over-excitement.

I walked away in stunned silence.

May 25 (Monday)

It was cold in Washington. The branch manager of All Nippon Airways came out to meet me. I could see his suspenders beneath his suit jacket. What a fashion-conscious Keio grad he is, I thought. We promised to play golf together soon before parting.

I reached my apartment just at noon. No sooner had I put my bags down than I walked next door to the Watergate Hotel, where I swam breaststroke for a thousand meters in the pool. I've found that this is the best way for me to cure jet lag!

In the evening, the telephone rang incessantly—in Tokyo, it was already the morning of May 26. "The financial world will support you." "I'll get up on the bandwagon in your support!" One after another, my friends kept calling to encourage me.

"Shall I give it a try?"—Just thinking about it made me forget decades, and my chest swelled up as though a yearning was boiling within.

"No, I don't think I'm cut out for it." Just thinking such a thing made me feel like a half-deflated balloon.

When Mr. Hosokawa finally called me, it was 3 AM. I found

myself saying, "All right; I'll take up the challenge," at which I felt a great sense of relief. After that, I slept like a log.

June 25 (Thursday)

ANA Flight 001 from Washington arrived at Tokyo's Narita Airport a whole forty-five minutes ahead of schedule at 2:10 PM. Some friends had come to greet me, and they gave me a bouquet of flowers.

June 26 (Friday)

"Everyone is coming to the meeting." The phone call was from the JNP campaign headquarters. It was 6 PM. "We'll all be there by 7 PM." So I hurriedly got ready and left the house.

Sitting around a table in a small, crowded conference room were fourteen men who had decided to propose a ticket centered around leader Morihiro Hosokawa. I wonder how many times these people over here in Japan have convened like this. This is my first time to join them, and I arrived late, so I felt a little uncomfortable.

On July 8, after the announcement of my candidacy, I went to a meeting where the laws governing campaign practices were to be explained to me. Since absolutely everything is new to me, I leaned forward, trying to take in all that was being said.

A pro from campaign headquarters was repeatedly saying that since this is an election of a person to represent the party, it would not do for individual personalities to get involved. "This is not allowed." "That is not allowed." He continued on and on in this vein so much that I started to think that there was nothing I do—that for me this campaign would mean nothing except being involved in PR activities.

All of the people there had come filled with enthusiasm and ready to get to work, but he was putting a damper on their ardor and casting a chill over the meeting.

June 29 (Monday)

Tonight, newscaster Yuriko Koike made with a flourish an official announcement of her candidacy with the JNP. Mentioning things such as the confused low prices on the Tokyo stock market, she seems to have a good sense of the state of things.

The people I meet ask me, "What's your running order?" But more than running in a particular order, I want to win. And in order to win, many believe that it's better for your name to appear near the top of the ballot. Perhaps everyone feels so.

June 30 (Tuesday)

I left my home in Tokyo's suburb of Kichijoji at 8 AM and went to the municipal center of the city of Musashino in order to obtain proof of residence. Until four years ago, I had been a resident of Musashino, but then, because I had gone to live in Washington, I now had to go back and re-register as a Musashino resident.

I had thought that the civil servants working at the city office would be unhelpful and haughty, but they were very kind, which surprised me. Although it seems they don't really start working until 8:30, and even though I had arrived early, a young woman who worked there (who had also arrived a little early). kindly made me a cup of tea. It seems that all the workers there have their own special cups—for drinking tea and coffee—of which they are very fond. It reminded me of when I was working for Nomura Securities. I used to drink my morning tea—which was delicious—out of tea cups bought especially for me by my female employees, who would buy me a cup or mug and then give it to me, saying, "Please use cup this for your tea."

At 10 AM, I met Mr. George Packard, Dean of the Johns Hopkins University School of Advanced International Studies (SAIS), at the Hotel Okura.

"I hear you're going to be a Senator. Congratulations!"

"No, it's too early for that. I'm only just starting to campaign."

Since being confirmed as a candidate, I've become aware that reactions of my Japanese friends are different from those of my American friends. All my American friends, for example, say things like, "I think it's wonderful!" and openly rejoice in my good fortune. Whereas the reactions of my Japanese friends are very difficult to describe, and all they say to me is the equivalent of something like, "Well, well. . . ."

Some even go on to say things like:

"You should be content to stay just the way you are. Why do you have to try to get a seat in the Senate?"

"Heaven knows you're far from being one of those dandies who would dye his hair black to hide his age or pin his Parliament badge prominently on his lapel whenever he went out, or stand in the most conspicuous spot whenever a photo was being taken, or have his name printed in ridiculously large letters on his name cards. . . ."

"Oh my! Are you going to join the ranks of the dirty politicians?"

"Ah, I think you should give it up—while you still can!"

Thus, in Japan it has come about that the ordinary person believes that an honest person would never consider becoming a politician. This is partly because our politicians, on whom the public has already turned its back out of a lack of trust, have assumed a much lower profile than is really necessary. Senators in the U.S. are as a matter of fact accorded respect by the general public.

At 3 PM, I happened to notice the President of the Okura, Mr. Gotoh, in the hotel's coffee shop. I called out to him and he turned around. He politely asked me when I had returned and how I was, but his expression was rather formal. I had not called to him with the intention of rallying his support for my campaign, but only because of the fond memories I have of our friendship over the years. But now I had managed unwittingly to strain that friendship—and for that I am truly sorry.

That night I had a phone call from Congressman Fumio Furuhashi (representative of the Lower House in the Japanese Diet) from my hometown of Sano in Tochigi prefecture. "The Governor of Tochigi would like you to resign from your position as Special Envoy "Marronier." (In Japanese, the word *tochigi* is the name of a kind of horse chestnut, and "chestnut tree" in French is *marronier*. Thus, as a kind of witty play on words, he had established the position of Special Envoy "Marronier," to which he appointed various people who had been born and raised in Tochigi prefecture—a novel idea that served as good PR for the prefecture. But since my becoming a candidate meant that my holding the post would be construed by some to give me a bias in favor of that prefecture, the Governor had no choice but to ask me to step down.

July 2 (Thursday)

At 7 AM, I went swimming at the Okura. Other regular members of the pool encouraged me, saying, "We'll root for you, so go for it!"

Later in the afternoon, I went out on an assignment for the *Washington Post* and the *Asahi Shimbun* newspapers.

Then at 4 PM, I visited the offices of Fuji Xerox, where I had an interview with Yotaro Kobayashi, who had lived in the same dormitory as me when we were students at the Wharton School of Business at the University of Pennsylvania.

At 6:30 PM, I went to a meeting of the "Society to Support Mr. Hosokawa" at Sogetsu Hall in Akasaka. I was surprised at the variety of people in attendance, including TV personality Françoise Moréchand, Olympic judo champion Yasuhiro Yamashita, environmental producer Man Arai, actress Yoko Shimada, and director Ben Wada.

July 3 (Friday)

At 6 AM, I called Mr. Louis Preston, President of the World Bank in Washington, where it was still 5 PM on July 2. "As of today, I am resigning my position as Executive Vice President of the Multilateral Investment Guarantee Agency (MIGA). Thank you very much for all your assistance during my term of office."

I think he stood perfectly still, silent while holding the receiver. I felt as though I could see the tall, broad-shouldered silhouette of Mr. Preston standing there as if he were an ice-hockey player waiting for the game to continue. . . .

July 4 (Saturday)

At 11 AM, I had a discussion with Mr. Tetsundo Iwakuni, Mayor of the city of Izumo, at a conference hosted by an international dyers' association at the Osaka Hilton. The theme of the gathering was "Japan as Seen by the World." Mr. Iwakuni, who knows me well, was very skillful at leading the discussion, and finally turned the topic to the inscrutable Japan that the world sees so much in recent times. The audience was made up of about 300 women, and I shook everyone's hand when it was over.

July 6 (Monday)

At 10 AM, there was a phone call from my party headquarters; my running order had been determined and they wanted to inform me of it—I was Number 3. Well, I thought, that's certainly a natural position for me (after both Mr. Hosokawa and Ms. Koike), so I gave my acceptance of that order. But now that that's been decided, it's time to start digging the trenches and to begin the fight!

July 8 (Wednesday)

I opened the window onto a fine summer's day. At last the day on which candidates are officially announced has come, and this campaign is starting full swing. But I still haven't even thought about what I'm going to say in my first speech. When things have come this far, all I can do is just go out there and hope to win or lose at this very moment.

At 10 AM, I went to Tokyo's Shibuya Station. When I passed by the statue of the faithful dog Hachiko, there were a number of loudspeaker-equipped trucks with people campaigning for many of the small parties, all with the volume turned up full blast!

The JNP was supposed to be near the South Exit, so I went over to the other side of the station, but all I could see were lots of TV cameras and reporters milling about—but there was no sign of the JNP campaign car. (And there was already enough ruckus going on with the sounds of the people from the media!)

"If Mr. Hosokawa doesn't get here before 10:30, I'll never meet the deadline for tonight's edition," whined a reporter dressed in red who was quite vociferous in her distress. But just then I happened to see Mr. Hosokawa coming, together with Ms. Koike.

The campaign car arrived. It seemed a lot smaller than those truck-sized vehicles on the Hachiko side of the station. It was just a small van with a place for a candidate to stand atop the roof. When Mr. Hosokawa stood up there, all the TV cameras turned to face him at once. Normally, he speaks in a rather quiet voice, but this morning he spoke with an effective raising and dropping of volume and with a slightly dramatic flair.

Then it was my turn and I got up on the roof of the van. Directly in front of me were seven or eight mikes, all taped together so that they resembled some weird bouquet. They made such a fat bundle one could just barely grasp it in both hands.

In the street were a lot of young men and women all dressed in rather flashy clothes, rushing here and there—all seemingly oblivious to our political rally. Despite that, I took a deep breath and began by saying, "I am Yoshio Terasawa of the Japan New Party." While talking, I saw my son Seido and my daughter Akiko and her husband (Mr. Yoneyama) standing in the crowd—so I waved at them.

I spoke of Japan's two leading parties, whose headquaters are located in Nagata-cho (Japan's Capitol Hill)—the Liberal Democratic Party (LDP), as being shaken with bribes and scandals; and the Social Democratic Party of Japan (SDPJ), as unrealistically following a dead ideology—and sharply criticized them, which to some degree helped to dissipate the anger I harbored toward them and made me feel better.

Not looking for very long at any single place, I kept turning my body to face here and there, as I had been advised by those with more experience at this sort of thing. Looking out over another crowd of people gathered to listen, I spotted my son's girlfriend and her mother. I wanted to tell them that my son was just over there, but I couldn't do such an indiscreet thing during my speech. I thought that when I was finished I would go over and tell them.

The weather was a little on the hot side, but it was cool enough to be comfortable. That evening, at 8 PM, I took a plane from Haneda to Sapporo.

July 9 (Thursday)

At 8 AM, I addressed the civil servants coming to work from atop a campaign car parked in front of the Hokkaido Prefectural Office. It might seem hasty, but I think I'm getting used to all this.

At 11 AM, I went canvassing all around Sapporo's Maruyama Stadium. That day, the baseball fans were bubbling with excitement over the game between Tokyo's Yomiuri Giants and Nagoya's Chunichi Dragons.

July 10 (Friday)

At 8 AM, I found myself in front of Japan Railways' Sannomiya Station, which is near Kobe. I campaigned in a loud voice, addressing all the men and women on their way to work from the station.

One person, an older man with a sunburnt, weather-beaten face got out of the train and approached—his rough appearance made me a little frightened. Without warning, he suddenly slapped me hard on the back and said, "Keep up the good work!" and he left us a small package filled with cans of ice-cold cola.

Shortly thereafter, a tall young man with a pale complexion came by, smiling. Saying, "This terrible heat is awful, isn't it. Oh, I don't mind if I do," he reached down and picked up one of the cans of cola the other man had left for us, and, without a word of thanks, he quickly walked away. Well, I guess the world is filled with all kinds of people!

That evening, I stayed at the Hotel Okura in Kobe.

July 11 (Saturday)

At 2:30 PM, I flew from Osaka's Itami Airport to Oita Airport in northeastern Kyushu. Then at 8 PM that evening, I met Mrs. Kayoko Hosokawa, wife of the party leader, at the Hotel Momiya in Beppu. She looks so much like him I thought that if someone turned Mr. Hosokawa into a woman this is what he'd look like! She is very intelligent and most charming. When I realized that we would be working together for a few days on a campaign tour of Kyushu, I was glad she was part of the tour.

July 13 (Monday)

While staying at ANA's Hotel Nikko Fukuoka in that northern Kyushu city, I received a call from a friend in Washington who said that there had been a large article in the July 12 edition of the *Washington Post* about my running for Senator. "This is incredible! I've lived in Washington for a long time, and I've never seen anything like this before. Even here, new movements on Japan's political scene are being closely watched."

July 14 (Tuesday)

We started our campaigning in Fukuoka City at 8 AM this morning. My friend and Waseda University classmate Minoru Koga, who had been born and raised in Fukuoka, came all the way from

Tokyo to make a speech in my support. He, of course, had planned to do his best to drum up support for me by appealing to the people in the local Fukuoka dialect. But a proper campaign should endeavor to sell the people on the merits of my party, the JNP, and not on me, the candidate. Of course, if you don't know who the candidate is, you can't vote for him; therefore, those running for office must all be people with the ability to pull in many votes. Thus, it is very difficult for candidates to fight for votes in an election within a system of proportional representation such as Japan's. And it seemed that his turn to speak would never come. Mr. Koga said, "That's all right," never once getting the chance to step out on the roof of the campaign car, and then put down a case of vitamin drinks for us and walked away. It seemed to me that his broad shoulders expressed his disappointment.

The mike was passed to Ms. Yuka Kawanami, from Keio University's Faculty of Law, who had come from Tokyo to volunteer her services. Just by having such a beautiful young woman like her stand there to speak, the entire atmosphere changed to one filled with gaiety. But still, I have to say to Mr. Koga that I'm very sorry he was never given the chance to speak.

"On election day," said Ms. Kawanami, "Vote for Japan's New Party!" Thus she concluded her speech, at the same time adding some personality to party politics. And she could say such a thing before such large crowds—she is really something!

Usually, when we finish campaigning in one place, the election car continues on and goes somewhere else. That day, the JNP's youngest candidate, Mr. Toshihiko Yokoo, was with us. As the car moved from place to place, he filled his speech with very appropriate ad libs geared toward gaining the support of the local people. For example, when we passed a scrap metal yard, he said, "Let's scrap old-fashioned politics and build up a new government!" And when we stopped in front of a gas station, he said, "Japan's government is ready for a change of oil—let's give it a new engine, too!" He is a student from the first class to graduate from the Matsushita Institute of Political Economy and is a very charismatic fellow.

That night, I flew back to Tokyo.

July 15 (Wednesday)

Today I took the day off. In the morning, I swam at the Hotel Okura pool. While I'm swimming, I always think that I'm lucky to be alive and happy. Later, when I got on the scales, I weighed in at 74 kg (163 lb). Only a month ago in Washington I had weighed 70 kg (154 lb)! That really threw a damper on my mood! I guess I have put on a little around the middle, but it won't do at all for me to get fat while I'm on the road on such a vigorous campaign tour. The thinner and more haggard I look the better! Oh, well. . . .

Later in the day I went to have my hair cut by my favorite barber, Mr. Yonekura. I always feel so relaxed while he's cutting my hair that I usually sleep through most of it.

July 16 (Thursday)

At 4 PM, I started campaigning in front of the Yurakucho Mullion Building with Yuriko Koike, Toshihiko Yokoo, and Yumiko Okawa. A soft breeze was gently blowing. To me, all the young and middle-aged women in the crowd seemed very pretty. The young women, especially, are looking more and more like American women these days. I got up on the roof of the campaign car and asked them: "Are you really satisfied with the way the government is operating in Japan today? Don't you think that we should try to do something to improve our overly slow-moving government? You should rise up in anger against it!" But my words left those listening unmoved.

But after stepping down from the car and shaking hands with everyone, many people gripped my hand tightly as they said things like, "We've had it with the LDP's shenanigans! Please do your best to defeat them!"

At 7 PM, there was a meeting of the party leadership at our headquarters in Tokyo's Takanawa. Now all the candidates who had carried out campaigns all over the country—from Hokkaido to Kyushu—had gathered together. We all exchanged comments and opinions gleaned from our campaigns during the one week since our candidacies had been officially announced.

I wonder whether our party will be able to secure enough votes? That's what everyone here is wondering. Nobody says a word about it, either, since nobody can predict what will happen. But party leader Mr. Hosokawa got up and said: "Your attention, please. I have an announcement to make." Then he introduced the story of how there had been a kind of fortune-telling session by using marbles. Someone had called together a group of 100 housewives and given each of them a bag of marbles. They were told to place the marbles in the containers representing the political party they wanted to vote for. They were also told that they could place as many marbles into as many containers as they wished. The result was that the JNP amassed some 530 marbles, leaving the LDP and JSP, which each gained a mere 100 or so, far behind. Smiling, Mr. Hosokawa said, "And surely this is how the elections will turn out for us!" Then all the candidates and staff workers forgot how tired they were and joined him in his cheerful smile.

July 17 (Friday)

I ran into Mr. Dan Cotton today at the Hotel Okura pool. We were both surprised. An American who acts as a business consultant, he now lives in Switzerland. He was once a lieutenant commander in the U.S. Navy—maybe that's why he's such a good swimmer! When I told him I was running for public office, his big eyes got even bigger. "That's great! We sure need someone like you who understands America in your parliament. . . . Well, it's too soon to congratulate you, but I wish you the best of luck and all the success in your campaign." Then he disappeared down the lane in a quick crawl.

July 18 (Saturday)

Something happened while I was campaigning in front of Sannomiya Station near Kobe today. Two young men started fighting. One of them caught the other in a crisp upper cut and sent him flying. He hit his head on a concrete wall and fell to the ground. I then used the loudspeakers to call the police for help. But Yuriko Koike then said in a loud, strident voice: "We should not be getting upset about such a trivial thing. Indeed, it is more important for us to rise up in anger against the dealings of our present government!"

July 26 (Sunday)

At 11 AM, my second daughter, Haruko, came running down the stairs. Huffing and puffing and out of breath, she said, "See you later!" But my wife said, "Of course, you're going to vote first," but she pouted, complaining that she was already late for her date. But she and my wife then went to the nearest voting station and cast their ballots.

On the news just now, they said that this election is drawing the lowest percentage of voters since the end of World War II. The weather is fine, but it's very humid. For a party like the JNP, which has no constituency, it hurts to hear that voter turnout is so low.

Later I went to the Kichijoji Community Center with my third daughter, Kuniko, and my eldest son, Seido. I saw many people carrying white postcards that had been mailed to them, telling them where they were to vote and proving their eligibility. Of course, I didn't have one, since I had only registered as a resident just under a month ago (and you must reside in a place continuously for at least three months before you can vote). So I stood by the entrance, waiting for my children to come back out. Only ten hours later we would all know whether or not I had won. Although I would like very much to be elected, I would also be rather relieved even if I lost.

Last night I was campaigning loudly from the roof of my campaign car in front of the east exit of Ikebukuro Station until about 8 PM. Actress Keiko Takeshita came with me to offer her support. Since it was a weekend, both men and women candidates (along with our staff) came attired in matching green polo shirts, even Ms. Takeshita. She looked like such an innocent young girl—it's hard to believe that she has two children of her own. I had asked several popular actress acquaintances of mine to join us, but, in the end, only Ms. Takeshita came.

I suppose that actresses must get a lot of requests from many different political parties and feel that to accept only some would not be fair, so they refuse to take part in all political rally events. That's what one of my actress friends told me. I guess that's the best way for them to get on in the world—by not doing anything that could offend many of their fans or sponsors.

But Keiko Takeshita, dressed in the same green polo shirt as the rest of us, got up on the roof of the campaign car and honestly and openly voiced her support for me and for the JNP. "I'm sure it won't offend the many companies in whose commercials I appear," she said, which made me worry about her all the more. Keiko—thank you very, very much. Yours is really a rarely found true friendship!

At 7 PM, we returned to the party headquarters. The building was surrounded by TV trucks, and the hall itself, which could comfortably seat about 200, was filled with cameramen and reporters from all the news media.

Together with five or six other candidates, I had dinner in a nearby hotel in Takanawa. I had consomme and steak. As the service at such places tends to be rather slow, we didn't order dessert and coffee until after 8 PM. Just about then, Mr. Kan-nari came rushing over from headquarters to tell us that Mr. Hosokawa had been successfully elected. We realized that we didn't have time for our dessert and coffee, and promptly returned to headquarters.

When we entered the hall, Mr. Hosokawa was standing there in the glare of TV lights and speaking softly into dozens of microphones.

In our headquarters, we had the names of the candidates all written on placards in large characters, and when the news came in that someone had been elected, a red rose was placed above the name—which presented a very different scene from that in the headquarters of other parties, in which you would find large papier-mâché dolls of the Buddhist patriarch Bodhidharma with only one eye painted in. (The other would be added when a candidate was elected.)

Four or five women wearing headphones that made them look like Martians were sitting at computer terminals, staring at the screens and pounding away at the keyboard incessantly. Now I'm all thumbs when it comes to anything mechanical, not knowing one thing from another, and I found myself gazing in wonder at all the pretty young "Martians" as they worked so hard.

At 9:15 PM, it was announced on NHK (Japan Broadcasting Corporation) TV that Yuriko Koike had also been elected. She was now on the Shinkansen ("Bullet Train") on her way back to Tokyo from Osaka. Thus, reporters were persistently asking the PR desk at our headquarters to tell them when she was expected to arrive. She flew by taxi directly from Tokyo Station to headquarters, and as soon as she arrived, she was surrounded by a forest of TV cameras and an explosion of flash bulbs.

On the NHK election results board, the number of JNP winners was posted as 2, and it seemed like it would remain 2 forever. We wondered if it would ever change to 3. If it stayed at 2, it would mean that I had failed.

Mr. Kanenari came over and whispered in my ear: "The Tokyo and Osaka polls have not yet closed. I'm sure it's just a matter of time before your election is confirmed." While waiting, I was surprisingly calm.

"How do you feel now?" reporters would ask.

"I'm confident that I will be elected, so I'm just quietly awaiting the results." I answered.

At 11:25 PM, someone—and I'm ashamed to say I don't remember now who it was—came over to me and said, "Mr. Terasawa. You have been elected." Now at last, it's over, I remember thinking. But I was wrong—it's only just begun!

Why I Ran for Public Office

For more than twenty years, I have periodically come home to Japan from my job in America—and each time I could not help thinking that there was something wrong with my country.

I wondered why ordinary Japanese, whose devotion to work in offices, factories, and homes was the primary factor in making Japan a world economic superpower, subject themselves to such miserable living conditions.

Some examples: In my old suburban Tokyo neighborhood of Kichijoji, the streets are only thirteen feet wide and lack sidewalks. When a car comes, you must flatten yourself against the wall to keep from getting run over.

I have relatives living in Ashikaga city, fifty miles north of Tokyo, whose house has no central heating, hot water, or flush toilets. This is a common feature of life beyond the biggest cities.

The truth is, people live much better in the United States, even with its budget and trade deficits, than people in Japan, whose economy boomed for years until the recession began a few months back.

An American friend who recently visited here observed the way we live and asked with genuine amazement, "Why isn't there a revolt in Japan?"

I didn't think about that conversation much at the time. But now I believe a revolution can occur in Japan—and I have decided to become part of it. I have left Washington, where I headed the World Bank's Multilateral Investment Guarantee Agency (MIGA), to run in the July 26 election for the upper house of the Japanese Diet (parliament) as a candidate from a newly formed political party.

I did this because I want to change the conditions in which we live—not only the physical conditions of our pressured, production-oriented lives, but the conditions of our psyches as well. By this I mean the pressure to conform, as well as what I consider the distorted and immature view we have of the world beyond our islands.

Japan undoubtedly has come a long way since my childhood, when we were all poor—but at least we ate dinner with our fathers. We now are one of the world's richest countries in terms of GNP, producing the highest-quality goods with utmost efficiency. But what is wealth if you can't enjoy it?

I touched above on some of the differences between Japanese and Americans. Here are more: Tokyo residents must drive hours in slow traffic to see trees and birds, while a mere half-hour from downtown Washington are beautiful suburbs full of charming houses set among tall trees—views seen only in the most exclusive resort communities in Japan. While residents of these Washington suburbs are not all that wealthy—perhaps earning about ¥10 million ($78,000) a year—Japanese with that income might never be able to own even a tiny condominium, much less a house.

In the supermarket, Tokyoites pay ¥235 for a kilogram of bananas, as opposed to ¥173 in Washington, ¥511 for a kilo of oranges vs. ¥199 in the United States; ¥383 per 100 grams of beef compared with ¥130 there. A family dinner at an ordinary restaurant would suck several ¥10,000 bills (approximately $160) out of papa's wallet, while an American family of four can get by for a month on $500 worth of groceries.

And even if one could afford it, there is no family life left in Japan anymore. On past visits home, I often called old friends at their offices around 10 PM—and in workaholic Japan, I always found them there. "How many times a week do you have dinner at home with your family?" I once asked a friend. He said, "Once or twice, perhaps."

These days, even the children don't come home till after 10 PM—they have to attend *juku,* cram schools, to prepare for entrance exams. This is because only one university counts here—the University of Tokyo, known as Todai. Children begin preparing to climb this Mount Fuji of all schools even before kindergarten, because a Todai diploma is the only sure passport to a good lifetime career.

In sixty years of living, I never once wanted to be a politician.

In fact, I particularly despise the Japanese breed of them. During my four years at MIGA and in thirty-four years at Nomura Securities before that (almost half of them in New York), I often felt ashamed of my country. But I never thought there was anything I, as an expatriate Japanese citizen, could do about it. I was content with a reasonably comfortable life for me and my family.

All that changed when I recently met Morihiro Hosokawa, an ex-member of the Diet and former governor of Kumamoto prefecture. Hosokawa had just launched a new political party, the Japan New Party, and asked me to run on its ticket in the July election. Despite my wife's vigorous opposition and strong counsel against it from friends who know something about Japanese politics, I decided to put off my retirement and bet my luck on Japan's future.

I was completely taken by Hosokawa's passion to pursue his ideals. A fifty-four-year-old descendant of the Kumamoto *daimyo,* or feudal lord, he convinced me that Japan desperately needs a new type of leadership that can steer the country into the role of a responsible player in international politics. The conventional parties, he said, have lost their ability to respond to the changes that have caught up with Japan and the world in the last few years. There is a ground swell of discontent among Japan's "silent majority," and people are crying out for a new political group that will truly represent the views of the ordinary Japanese citizen, not just those of special interest groups or the status quo. Everything he said made sense.

I now feel it's my destiny to use my experience in running an international organization and my twenty-one years of living in the United States to prepare Japan for the twenty-first century. If elected to an at-large seat, I will work hard to mend Japan's relationship with the United States, which has deteriorated to the lowest point I can remember. Japan must quit hiding behind the United States and start saying what it thinks about international issues, and it needs to open its domestic market to foreign goods, and fulfill its responsibilities as the second-richest country in the world. I will try my best to make the Japanese people understand this, while keeping in close touch with American lawmakers.

I would also like to overhaul the Japanese educational system in order to nurture a generation of Japanese who are true cosmopolitans. It is absurd to sacrifice one's childhood solely for the prestige of a Todai degree. We must put less emphasis on conformity and uniformity, and more on creativity and freedom of choice.

But most importantly, I would like to take Japanese politics away from the traditional party politicians, who are in bed with the big corporations and interest groups, and put our politics back in the hands of consumers and ordinary citizens. This is the path to genuine improvement of domestic life and conditions for our citizens.

Japanese political pros tell me I am too naive in thinking that a small new party can make any difference in how the country operates. They may be right. But I reply to them, "Let's wait until the year 2000. Japan may have changed a little bit by then, thanks to us amateurs."